# Hands-On Intranets

*Vasanthan S. Dasan*
*Luis R. Ordorica*

***Sun Microsystems Press***
***A Prentice Hall Title***

The publisher offers discounts on this book when ordered in bulk quantities. For more information, contact Corporate Sales Department, Prentice Hall PTR, One Lake Street, Upper Saddle River, NJ 07458.
Phone: 800-382-3419; FAX: 201-236-7141.
E-mail: corpsales@prenhall.com.

Editorial/production supervision: *Nicholas Radhuber*
Cover designer: *M&K Design, Palo Alto, California*
Cover design director: *Jerry Votta*
Manufacturing manager: *Alexis R. Heydt*
Marketing manager: *Stephen Solomon*
Acquisitions editor: *Gregory G. Doench*
Sun Microsystems Press publisher: *Rachel Borden*

10 9 8 7 6 5 4 3 2 1

ISBN 0-13-857608-4

**Sun Microsystems Press**
**A Prentice Hall Title**

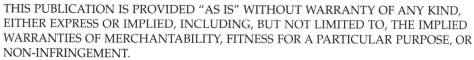

***Sun Microsystems Press***
**A Prentice Hall Title**

*To Priya, Naren, and my mother.*
*Vasanthan*

*To Karen, Briony, and Mom.*
*Luis*

# Contents

---

# Part 1: Introduction

## Chapter 4

# Firewall and Proxy Services, 37

## Chapter 5

## Part 3: Building the Services Infrastructure

## Chapter 18
# The Common Gateway Interface, 279

# Foreword

Companies are now spending more of their IT budgets on intranets than on the Internet in general, and this is expected to double by the year 2000.

Why are organizations looking at intranets? ROI, (Return On Investment): increased efficiency and lowered costs of operations. These are found in all areas, not the least of which is retiring proprietary systems and interfaces and replacing them with easy to use web-based front-ends and standards-based infrastructures that can run in a heterogenous environment. And some companies are seeing more than 1,000% positive ROI in a matter of weeks after deployment, not months or years.

In the first year that Sun moved to a consistent and unified intranet organization, we saved over $25 million. We turned instantly obsolete 400-page paper price books into online web pages for our field staff with dynamic product information. We replaced proprietary human resource and help systems with easily updatable HTML-based tools.

Your organization can also save money, reduce costs, and increase productivity. And, as an organization moves from just sharing information on the intranet to the next stage of dynamic collaborative transactions, the efficiencies can really pay off. This book can help you get there.

*Hands-On Intranets* is a comprehensive guide to what the elements of intranets are and provides step-by-step details for setting up an intranet in your location. It is written in an approachable and practical manner, with all you need to start implementing an intranet. The eminently pragmatic approach taken by the authors is a testament to their pioneering work done in implementing Sun's own intranet structure.

Bill Petro
Marketing Development Director
International Marketing
Sun Microsystems, Inc.

# Preface

Corporations are abandoning computing environments based on costly proprietary technologies and adopting *intranets*—open, standards-based computing environments based on technologies such as TCP/IP. Vendors are responding to this shift by integrating standards-based technologies into their products. For example, Microsoft has provided support for TCP/IP in the Windows 95 operating system (OS) environment.

A systems and network administrator tasked with building an intranet faces a new set of problems. Because an intranet is based on a heterogenous computing environment, an extensive skill set is required. For example, many popular intranet services can be hosted on servers running the UNIX OS environment, and the administrator must understand how these services are implemented in this OS. Similarly, since most intranet services are accessed by desktop clients running either Windows 95 or Windows NT, the administrator must also be proficient in these OS environments.

The intranet administrator's job is to install, configure, monitor, and troubleshoot a heterogenous computing environment, in addition to other important activities, such as training end-users and writing administration procedures. This can be a daunting endeavor, especially since the nature of the intranet requires broad cross-platform administrative skills.

Many system administrators who are well-versed in the nuances of a particular computing environment are faced with the challenge of learning new skills in order to keep pace with the changing corporate computing landscape. For all of the advantages it brings, the heterogeneity the intranet introduces into the enterprise requires new administrative knowledge and skills.

This book is a guide to administering an intranet. Our goal is to guide you through the process of setting up and maintaining an intranet using narration, examples, and hands-on activities. We'll describe essential intranet services, and then we'll walk you through the tasks required to establish these services in a step-by-step manner. We'll also tell you where to find more information on the Web wherever this is appropriate.

Our focus is the interoperability of the Solaris, Windows 95, and Windows NT operating environments. Although there are many books that describe the specifics of each OS environment in an intranet setting, there is a need for a book that describes how to set up an intranet comprised of all three OS environments. In this book, we'll show you how to integrate the protocols and services available for the Solaris OS environment with a network comprised of clients and servers running Windows 95 and Windows NT.

This book also shows the path to adopting the TCP/IP standard in the enterprise, and it explains how to achieve the intranet promise of better communication and lower costs. For example, we'll look at how to access legacy information sources in an intranet.

## Audience

This book is primarily intended for system and network administrators who have some experience installing and administering an OS environment such as Solaris or Windows 95. It also contains useful information for the IS manager. Besides these two groups, this book should be helpful to end-users seeking to understand how an intranet works.

## Conventions Used In This Book

The table below shows the typographic conventions used in this book.

**Typographic Conventions**

| Typeface or Symbol | Description |
| --- | --- |
| `courier` | Indicates a command, file name, HTML tag, or file content. |
| **`bold courier`** | Indicates a sample command-line entry. |
| *italics* | Indicates definitions, emphasis, a book title, or a variable you should replace with a valid value. |
| ➤ | Indicates a menu item you should choose. |

Unless otherwise noted, the term Windows applies to both the Windows 95 and Windows NT OS environments.

# Acknowledgments

This book would not have been possible without the encouragement, advice, and help from many individuals. First, we'd like to thank Alan McClellan for inspiring us to take on this project and for his help reviewing the materials. We also owe thanks to our other reviewers, including Bill Petro, Will Snow, and especially Peter Gregory, who provided us with excellent ideas on how to best organize the information in the book.

We also would like to thank management for supporting us in our endeavour. This includes Randy Kalmeta, Lynn Rohrer, Ken Kadonaga, and Beth Papiano. There are many other friends at Sun whom we would like to acknowledge, including Paul Kasper, Mike Jessie (third base coach), Rick Ramsey, Randy Crihfield, Mike Gionfriddo, Russ Chang, and Scott Hudson.

Thanks also goes to Rachel Borden of Sun Microsystems Press for believing in us and giving us the opportunity to work with her. John Bortner also deserves our thanks for providing us with excellent support. We'd also like to thank Greg Doench and Nick Radhuber of Prentice Hall.

Finally, we'd like to thank our wives and families for putting up with all the late nights and weekends we spent working on the book. Their patience and love made all the difference.

# List of Tables

# *List of Code Examples*

# List of Figures

# Hands-On
# Intranets

# Introduction

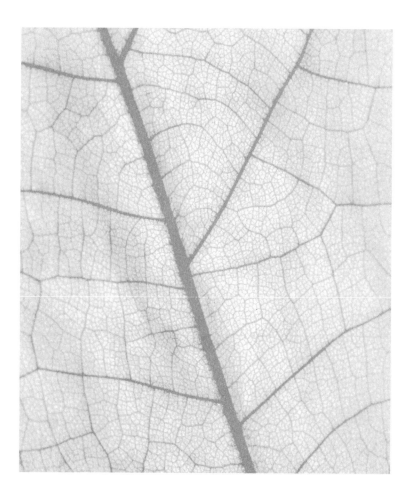

# CHAPTER 1

# Introduction

## What is an Intranet?

At its core, an intranet is a heterogenous computing environment that promotes the exchange of information. This information exchange occurs among different hardware platforms, but more importantly, the exchange is between different operating system environments.

This book focuses on the following operating system environments:

- Solaris 2.$x$

- Windows NT Version 4.0

- Windows 95

### A Heterogenous Computing Environment

In a typical intranet computing environment, you will find different hardware platforms, different operating system environments, and different window system environments (user interfaces) seamlessly communicating and exchanging data.

### An Open, Client / Server Computing Environment

An intranet is also an example of client/server computing. Information processing is distributed, with the client cooperating with the server to perform computing tasks over the network.

To illustrate how the client/server computing model is used in the intranet, consider the following scenario. An intranet user wants to see how his or her retirement savings funds are performing. Luckily, this information is available on a corporate web site, and all the user has to do in order to access the records is start a web browser and visit the web site.

Here is a breakdown of the events that occur between the web browser client and the web server hosting the web site.

- The web browser requests a page containing a retirement savings balance request form from the web server over the network.

- A process running on the web server processes the request, and sends the page containing the form encoded in HTML to the requestor.

- The web browser interprets the HTML instructions, and renders the retirement savings balance request form on screen. The form contains empty fields for the user's name, password, and user ID.

- The user completes the fields in the form, and presses the Submit button.

- The web server authenticates the user by verifying the user name and password are correct, and then processes the request by passing the input to a CGI program.

- The CGI program running on the web server process the input, and queries the retirement savings database. The results of the query are formatted in HTML and sent to the web browser.

- The web browser renders the query results on screen, and the user is presented with his or her retirement savings fund balances.

The web client/server interaction in our scenario is illustrated in Figure 1-1.

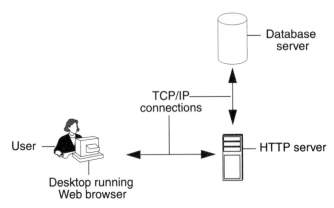

**Figure 1-1** Example — Web Client / Server Interaction

The web browser, web server, and database used in this scenario could potentially be running on different types of computers using different operating system environments, such as Windows or Solaris. Since they all use a common communication medium, the Transmission Control/Internet Protocol (TCP/IP), they work together seamlessly as a unified system. This is an example of the interoperability you can achieve in a diverse and heterogenous computing environment, and it is a significant intranet advantage.

### A Network Computing Environment for the Corporation

An intranet is the ideal network computing environment for the corporation because it lowers the cost of managing and providing information services. Since the intranet is not tied to a particular brand of operating system environment or computing platform, you can select among competing vendors for the one that best meets your needs. An open, standards-based computing environment also means never being locked into expensive, proprietary technologies. A heterogenous computing environment enables users to work productively, regardless of their choice of computing platform, and a client/server architecture allows you to scale information services to meet the growing needs of your organization.

### Intranet Services

An intranet service encourages the seamless exchange of information, which can be the most important asset for an organization. You will find the following services in most intranets:

- Name services

  Name services (also known as directory services) provide clients with addresses for printers, users, hosts, networks, and other types of information needed to perform common intranet activities such as printing, web browsing, sending e-mail, and so on. For example, the Domain Name Service (DNS) is used in an intranet to provide Internet Protocol (IP) addresses for hosts.

- Electronic mail (e-mail) services

  This service supports the exchange of electronic messages based on open, standards-based protocols such as the Simple Mail Transfer Protocol (SMTP), the Interactive Mail Access Protocol (IMAP4), and the Post Office Protocol (POP3) protocols. E-mail is historically thought of as the exchange of simple ASCII text messages, but it can be extended to include richer information types such as audio, images, and pointers to web sites.

- File sharing services

  A file sharing service enables remote file system access. With file sharing, files are stored on a remote computer, but they are accessed as if they reside on the local computer. File sharing usually requires a high bandwidth network, such as a LAN. Either commercial or public domain software can be used to provide file sharing services. For example, Solstice Network Client is a SunSoft product that enables users to share files in a Solaris and Windows computing environment. A public domain product, Samba, enables users to share files in a Windows-only environment.

- Printing services

  Using a print service, users submit requests or print jobs for hard copy versions of electronic documents. The print service is implemented as a process running on a server that receives print jobs. The print server can receive print jobs in a heterogenous fashion using an open printing service such as `lpr`. The print job is created on the print client system (for example, a Windows 95 desktop), and it is submitted to the print server for processing.

- Web services

  As we mentioned earlier, a web service is based on a client/server model for accessing and providing information. Using a web browser on the client, users can easily navigate through the information space using hypertext links embedded with Universal Resource Locators (URL). A URL is an address that specifies the location of a file on a server, as well as the protocol used to access the file.

- Software distribution services

  This service can include the distribution of platform-specific software applications, such as office productivity application software. The server can provide the latest version of the software that is pre-configured, license-enabled, and customized for the user. All these capabilities are provided using the intranet.

- Data exchange/database access services

  An example of this service is a client/server application that accesses and makes changes to the information stored on an SQL database. Using a web browser interface, clients can access the database to request and store information.

- Specialized services

  A specialized service is a specialized file-based service such as Usenet news. The client contacts the server in a specific fashion and requests the file using a specific protocol, such as the Network News Transfer Protocol (NNTP). The server returns the file with a specific header, format, and so on.

## Why Intranets?

Here are a few questions to ask yourself to help you decide if your company needs an intranet.

- Does your company use several different types of computers and different operating system environments?

- Do your users need access to company information such as policies, announcements, memos, and so on?

- Do you want to manage information in a centralized and easy-to-access manner?

- Are users demanding more autonomy in accessing and publishing information?

- Do you want to reduce the amount of time you spend administering platform-specific software?

If you answered affirmatively to three or more of the above, then it is likely that your company can benefit from an intranet. Let's look in more detail at the benefits an intranet can bring to your organization.

## Intranet Benefits

There are several advantages the intranet brings to your organization. These benefits are improved internal and external communications, reduced cost of ownership, and better interoperability.

### Improved Communications

The central theme and benefit to all intranet services is that they are heterogenous and client/server based. The result is an enabling computing environment for users, with better communication between the people who work in the organization and better communication outside of the organization. Information tends to flow more freely in an intranet. Because users can easily access and publish information using web services, they have more control. Individuals seeking information are no longer required to use arcane access methods—the data they need is just a few mouse clicks away using a web browser. With e-mail services, information can be communicated instantaneously to small or large audiences. The distribution of information mimics and complements the decentralized nature of most organizations in an intranet.

Because communication is based on relatively simple and open standards, such as ASCII and HTML, communication is improved outside of the organization as well. Customer-oriented functions such as marketing and service are improved by opening up access to internal databases, for example. Work flow processes with business partners are also improved. For example, an organization that uses an outside publishing company to produce bound versions of technical manuals can reduce production times by transferring files electronically to the vendor.

### Reduced Cost of Ownership

The cost of distributing information in an intranet is usually much less than traditional methods. Since the infrastructure of an intranet is based on open standards found in the Internet (such as TCP/IP), an intranet is more flexible and less costly than a proprietary Network Operating System (NOS) environment.

A NOS-based environment is expensive to own, since it requires investment in proprietary software (such as protocol stacks and applications) and hardware (such as file servers that work only in the NOS environment). Such an environment can also be expensive to maintain over time. When compared with the cost of owning a TCP/IP network, the advantage is clear. The cost of owning a TCP/IP network can be as little as 15% of owning a NOS-based network, which is a significant advantage.

Since TCP/IP is an open network standard that encourages innovation and competition among vendors, there is a substantially larger set of applications available for TCP/IP networks. Intranet applications that utilize intranet services such as web services and e-mail operate using TCP/IP connections. To use these applications in a NOS environment, it would require a significant porting effort to enable them to operate over proprietary NOS protocols. Almost all major operating system environments offer built-in TCP/IP support, but very few support a proprietary NOS out of the box.

Intranets, when properly designed, enable cost savings through the centralization of services on servers. A centralized service environment is easier and cheaper to administer than an environment where services and resources are haphazardly distributed, which unfortunately has been the case for many environments using personal computers.

Another cost savings benefit arises from lower employee training costs. Most intranet services are based upon ubiquitous and easy-to-use applications used in the Internet, such as a web browser. These end-user application skills are easily learned, and they can be quickly adapted for other uses.

### Better Interoperability

In the open, TCP/IP-based network, a client-side application can be built for a particular platform that communicates and interoperates with a server-side application on a different platform, without requiring the client to know the specifics of the server implementation, and vice-versa. This concept is illustrated in Figure 1-2.

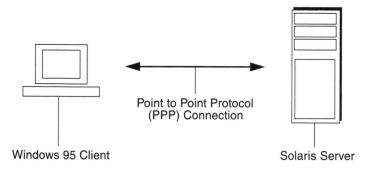

Point to Point Protocol
(PPP) Connection

Windows 95 Client                        Solaris Server

**Figure 1-2** TCP/IP Enables Heterogenous Client / Server Interoperability

Interoperability is enabled for network-based applications, such as the web browser, as illustrated in Figure 1-3.

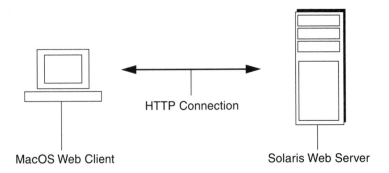

**Figure 1-3** TCP/IP Enables Heterogenous Client / Server Applications

Besides enabling interoperability among varying platforms, operating system environments, and applications, TCP/IP offers a compelling list of advantages:

- TCP/IP is ubiquitous.

  TCP/IP is available natively as part of the standard feature set in Windows, Solaris and other UNIX variants, MacOS, and other operating environments.

- TCP/IP is reliable.

  TCP/IP is a reliable and robust protocol with built-in error detection and recovery capabilities.

- TCP/IP is based on standards.

  The Internet Engineering Task Force (IETF) standards body, and not a corporation, governs the TCP/IP standard.

- TCP/IP has multi-vendor support.

  TCP/IP is available for all types of operating environments, from portable digital assistants (PDA) all the way up to mainframes.

- TCP/IP has lower development costs.

  Developers don't have to customize a service for a particular platform, for example. Instead, they develop for the protocol based on TCP/IP, such as Winsock, BSD sockets, and so on, and the applications they write are backward compatible.

- TCP/IP is scalable.

  TCP/IP has accommodated the growth of the Internet from just a few nodes to a world-wide network comprised of millions of connected computers. It is protocol that is embraced by many vendors and operating system environments.

- TCP/IP has lower administrative costs.

  Most vendors build in administration tools with their TCP/IP products.

- TCP/IP promotes seamless communication and data exchange.

- TCP/IP supports a common set of services:
  - File services.
  - E-mail services.
  - Print services.
  - Network management services.
  - Directory services.
  - Web services.

- TCP/IP is the corporate computing environment of choice.

  Industry experts predict that by the year 2000, all corporate networks will be based on TCP/IP.

## Intranet Implementations

The infrastructure, applications, and services found in an intranet will vary based on the implementation. Generally speaking, intranets fall into two types of categories: commercial intranets and non-commercial intranets.

### *Commercial Intranets*

Besides the attributes we mentioned earlier (such as the emphasis on open, standards-based protocols and services), a commercial intranet tends to exhibit the following characteristics:

- Security

  An organization must protect its information assets and take steps to prevent unauthorized access to information resources and services. Care must be taken when configuring remote access for roaming employees, for example.

- Focused heterogeneity

  Some companies try to limit the heterogeneity of the computing environment by creating standards. A standards-based environment promotes the use of similar hardware platforms, operating system environments, software applications, and so on. This practice falls under the official guise of curtailing growing IS management costs, but it can be difficult to enforce if employees have strong preferences for certain brands that fall outside the company standard.

- Commercial applications

  Companies that depend on software applications to perform basic business functions require support levels typically not found in public domain software, such as customer support, documentation, and so on. They usually invest in fully-supported, commercial application software.

### Non-Commercial Intranets

A non-commercial intranet is usually an environment where security is important but not critical. The best example of a non-commercial intranet is the university environment. Here are some of the characteristics that are common to this environment:

- Heterogenous computing

  You will find large numbers of PC and Macintosh users in a university setting.

- Non-commercial applications

  The types of computing activities are centered around research and development, training, and education.

- Heavy use of public domain software

  Low-cost software that does not require high support levels appeals to university intranet users.

## Summary

In this chapter, we've defined the intranet, and described the characteristics that make it the ideal computing environment for the corporation. We listed the benefits of the intranet for your organization, and we discussed how an open, standards-based computing environment costs less to own and enables communication across an array of computer platforms and operating system environments. In later chapters, we'll describe techniques and strategies you can use to set up and effectively manage the core services that comprise your intranet. Ultimately, our goal is to show you how to provide a wealth of information services to your users, which enables them to make better business decisions on a day-to-day basis, and leads to a significant competitive advantage for your organization.

# CHAPTER

## 2

# Intranets, Big and Small

An intranet has something to offer for organizations of all types and sizes. In this chapter, we'll show you examples of how intranet services can be used in a small, medium, and large company. You should be able to find similarities between the companies we describe in this chapter and your company. This will help to give you an idea of the scope of your intranet needs, and it will also provide you with a frame of reference for the topics described in the chapters to come.

## Organizational Growth and Intranet Service Levels

As an organization grows, many factors contribute to the number and level of intranet services that it requires, such as:

- Number of employees
- Geographical locations
- Business functions
- Remote sites
- Distributed offices
- "Roaming" employees

Figure 2-1 describes three sizes of intranets based on the number of employees and cost.

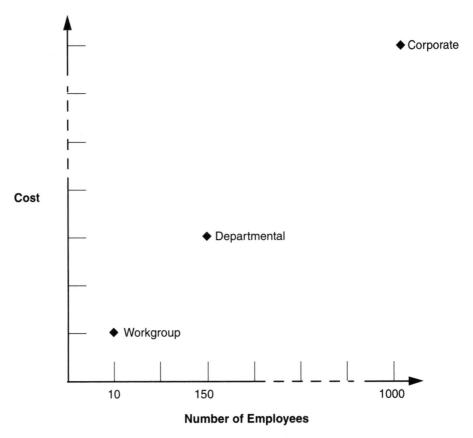

**Figure 2-1** Intranet Size by Cost and Number of Employees

Fortunately, the inherent flexibility of the services provided within an intranet can easily be scaled to accommodate the growth of an organization. Let's look at some examples of how an intranet scales to meet the needs of the workgroup, department, and corporation.

## The Workgroup Intranet

### *Graphic Design Company*

XYZ Graphics is a small company that provides graphic design services to its clients. XYZ Graphics creates artwork such as logos, advertisements, and so on. The employees of XYZ Graphics use an assortment of 2-D and 3-D graphics design software, and also office productivity applications such as word processing and accounting software packages.

Here is a sampling of the daily intranet activities at XYZ Graphics:

- Use e-mail to exchange ideas
- Share designs, logos, and graphic template files
- Review artwork with customers
- Communicate with customers in a timely fashion

The company has a small Ethernet-based local area network, and its size and other attributes are described below.

**Table 2-1** Workgroup Example – Company Attributes

|  | Description | Number |
|---|---|---|
| Company size | Employees | 7 |
|  | Geographical locations | 1 |
|  | Business functions | 1 |
|  | Remote sites | — *none* — |
|  | Dedicated system administrators | — *none* — |
| Computing infrastructure | Servers | 1 |
|  | Desktops | 5 |
|  | Printers | 1 |

Even though it is a small organization, XYZ Graphics relies on core intranet services described in Table 2-2 that are common to intranets of all sizes.

**Table 2-2** Workgroup Example – Intranet Services

| Service | Description |
|---|---|
| File Sharing | Company data is centralized. Employees work on data files stored locally on each desktop system. After working on the files, they are copied to the central file server, which is backed up regularly. |
| File Transfer | Though the company is not directly connected to the Internet, it transfers artwork to clients using a dial-up connection to a subscription based Internet Service Provider (ISP). |
| E-mail | E-mail access is provided by the ISP, and it is the primary form of communication with company clients. |
| Printing | Print jobs are transferred over the network to a PostScript printer. |

XYZ Graphics derives two important benefits from its intranet—file sharing and transfer, and e-mail. Without these intranet services, the company would be forced to use other methods to get work done, such as exchanging files using floppy disks and other removable media, and using traditional means for business correspondence, such as snail-mail.

The cost savings come from shorter development times due to more efficient file access and transfer methods, and an overall improvement in business communications resulting in a shorter business cycle.

## The Departmental Intranet

### Personnel Recruitment Agency

ABC Financial Recruiters is a mid-sized company that recruits finance professionals for its clients, large financial corporations seeking to fill open positions including financial analysts, portfolio managers, and stock traders. ABC employees track information such as job openings, resumes, required skills, and salary requirements using a central database. The database is accessed from the desktop computer of every employee using a web browser interface. Employees continually update records stored in the database, and they run programs that try to match people seeking work with employers.

The company has a large Ethernet-based local area network at the corporate site, and it is connected to remote sites using leased lines or ISDN. The company's size and other attributes are described below.

**Table 2-3** Departmental Example – Company Attributes

|  | Description | Number |
|---|---|---|
| Company size | Employees | 75 |
|  | Geographical locations | 1 |
|  | Business functions | 1 |
|  | Remote sites | 2 |
|  | Distributed offices | 3 |
|  | Dedicated system administrators | 1 |
| Computing infrastructure | Servers | 2 |
|  | Printers | 8 |

| Description | Number |
|---|---|
| Desktops | 60 |
| Printers | 8 |

ABC Financial Recruiters uses the intranet services described in Table 2-4.

**Table 2-4** Departmental Example – Intranet Services

| Service | Description |
|---|---|
| File sharing | Company data is centralized. Employees work on data files stored centrally on the server that is backed up regularly. |
| File transfer | Files are exchanged with external organizations using a direct Internet connection. |
| E-mail | E-mail access is provided by a direct Internet connection. |
| Printing | Print jobs are transferred over the network to PostScript printers. |
| Web | A web server running custom common gateway interface (CGI) programs provides access to the central database from a web browser interface. |

Unlike the workgroup intranet example, this company has connectivity needs that require more bandwidth than is provided using dial-up Internet services. To meet this need, the company uses an Internet Access Provider (IAP). The IAP provides a direct connection to the Internet using a dedicated 56Kb T1 line. Usage and maintenance costs are billed to the company on a monthly basis.

# The Corporate Intranet

## Computer Manufacturing Company

PQR Systems is a large computer manufacturing company. Like many large corporations, there is a variety of business functions performed at the company, such as engineering, sales and marketing, customer service, and so on. The needs of each functional organization add to the overall level of service required in the intranet.

The company has a wide area network it uses to connect a series of Ethernet-based local area networks. The WAN is managed by a common carrier, while LANs, or subnets, are managed internally. The company's size and other attributes are described below.

**Table 2-5** Corporate Example – Company Attributes

|  | Description | Number |
|---|---|---|
| Company size | Employees | 1000 |
|  | Geographical locations | 3 |
|  | Business functions | 5 |
|  | Remote sites | 3 |
|  | Distributed offices | 20 |
|  | Dedicated system administrators | 50 |
| Computing infrastructure | Servers | 20 |
|  | Desktops | 900 |
|  | Network Computers | 100 |
|  | Printers | 50 |

PQR Systems uses the intranet services described in Table 2-6.

**Table 2-6** Departmental Example – Intranet Services

| Service | Description |
|---|---|
| Software distribution | Application software is distributed using a file sharing service wherever possible. |
| OS installation | Operating system software is installed using automated methods wherever possible. |
| Home directory | Access to user-specific file storage is provided using a file sharing service. |
| Directory | The Domain Name Service (DNS) is used to provide host name lookup services. |
| Security | A firewall service protects the company from external attacks. |
| Remote access | Dial-up remote access services based on the Point-to-Point Protocol (PPP) are provided to roaming and off-site users. |
| File sharing | Company data is centralized. Employees use the Network File System (NFS) distributed file system to work on data files stored centrally on the server that is backed up regularly. |
| File transfer | Files are exchanged with external organizations using a direct Internet connection managed through a firewall. |
| E-mail | E-mail services are provided internally using mail servers. |

**Table 2-6** Departmental Example – Intranet Services (Continued)

| Service | Description |
|---|---|
| Printing | Print jobs are transferred over the network to PostScript printers. |
| Web | Web servers running custom Common Gateway Interface (CGI) programs provides access to legacy databases from a web browser interface. |
| Web proxies | Caching web proxy servers provide users with access to external web sites and help distribute the network load. |

As you can see, a larger organization has a greater dimension of intranet needs. Some of the problems that intranet services address in a corporation, such as remote access, simply don't exist in the workgroup-sized intranet, for example.

## Summary

The services used in the typical workgroup, departmental, and corporate intranet are the foundation for the topics described in this book. We'll describe each intranet service in much more detail, and explain the particular problem that is addressed by the service. Our goal is to provide you with background information for an intranet service, along with examples and step-by-step procedures wherever possible to help you set up and manage services in your intranet. We'll also tell you where you can find more information on a particular topic on the Web or from other sources.

# Building the Network Infrastructure

**PART TWO**

# CHAPTER

## 3

# Networking Basics

In this chapter, we'll briefly describe networking concepts to give you a basic understanding of how computers communicate over a network using TCP/IP. We will discuss the TCP/IP networking model and network protocols, and we'll show how applications use TCP/IP to exchange data with other computers over the network. Finally, we'll introduce tools you can use to analyze network activity in a TCP/IP network.

## Network Models

A *network* is a collection of computers and other devices that are connected in some manner. In an intranet, this could represent desktop computers, server systems, and printers connected together using ethernet. *Networking* is the collection of activities that occur in order for computers to exchange data reliably. Networking can be visualized as a layered model in which each layer performs a specific function and passes control to the next layer. Networking theory refers to the seven-layer OSI model shown in Figure 3-1.

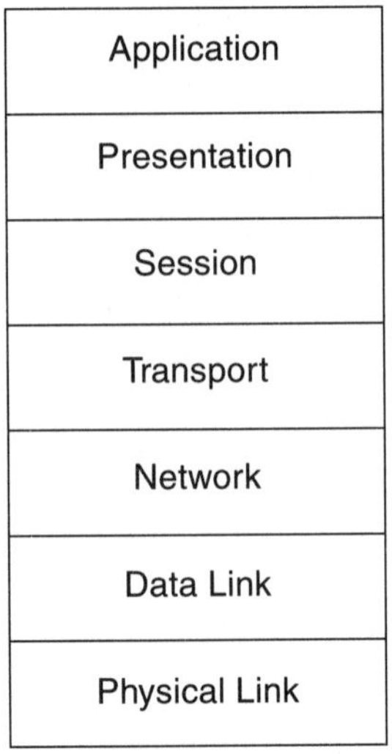

| Application |
| --- |
| Presentation |
| Session |
| Transport |
| Network |
| Data Link |
| Physical Link |

**Figure 3-1** OSI Network Model

In practice, not all layers are strictly enforced. For example, the TCP/IP model is a simplification of the OSI model that can be conceptualized with five layers, as shown in Figure 3-2.

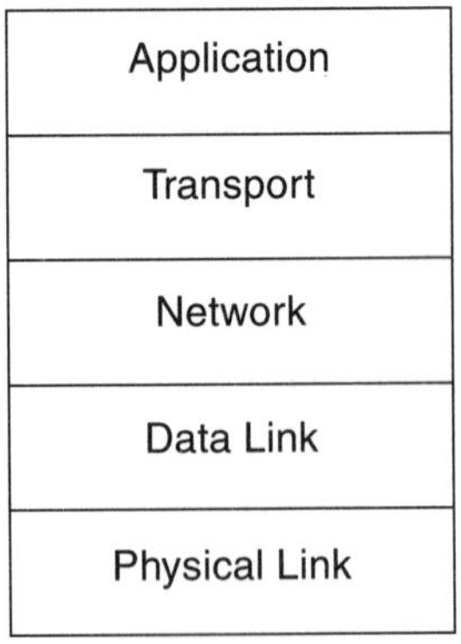

| Application |
| --- |
| Transport |
| Network |
| Data Link |
| Physical Link |

**Figure 3-2** TCP/IP Network Model

Let's look at the types of networking activities that occur at each layer in the TCP/IP model:

- Application layer

  The application layer is responsible for defining how cooperating networks represent data. Example applications include web browsers, Telnet, FTP, NFS, and so on.

- Transport layer

  The transport layer manages the transfer of data using acknowledgments and no acknowledgments of transport protocols. The transport layer is also responsible for managing connections (set up and tear down) between cooperating applications.

- Network layer

  The network layer is responsible for data addressing and delivery of packets. A packet is a self-contained unit of information that is constructed by the sending computer and sent over the network to the destination computer.

- Data link layer

  The data link layer manages packet delivery.

- Physical link layer

  The physical link represents networking hardware and interconnections. Examples include network interface cards and network hubs.

## Communicating over the Network Using TCP/IP

TCP/IP uses packet-switching to enable computers to exchange data over the network. In a packet-switching network, packets traveling to the same destination may use a number of different routes over the network. To explain this concept, we'll use the scenario shown in Figure 3-3.

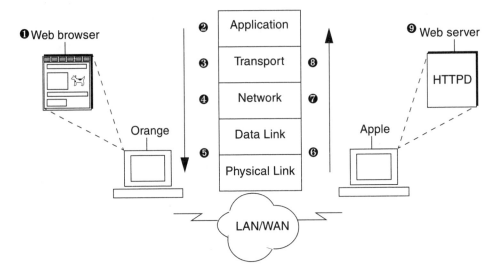

**Figure 3-3** TCP/IP Network Transaction

In this scenario, the web browser application running on orange wishes to load a web page hosted by the HTTPD server process running on apple. This request is managed over the network using TCP/IP. Let's examine the network activities that must occur to support this transaction:

❶   orange sends an HTTP request to apple.

❷   The request is assembled by the application layer and passed on to the transport layer.

❸   The transport layer then partitions the request into TCP packets and pads them with source/destination information, and sends it to the network layer.

❹   The network layer chooses the next destination of the packet (in a series of hops) and sends it down to the interface which sends it via the networking hardware over the wire.

❺   The packets are routed using several network interfaces.

❻   The packets arrive at the destination's network interface, and they are processed from the bottom layer up.

❼   The packets are filtered by the network layer.

❽   The packets are re-assembled by transport layer.

❾   The request is passed on to the HTTPD daemon for processing.

Note that this process occurs for each individual packet. A single request may consist of several packets, and each packet may take a different path or *route* to its final destination. Routing occurs dynamically, and it is managed in the network layer.

### TCP and UDP

Both the Transmission Control Protocol (TCP) and User Datagram Protocol (UDP) transport protocols are available in the transport layer. The basic difference between the two is the manner in which reliability is guaranteed. Upon assembly of each TCP packet, the transport layer sends an acknowledgment of the packet's receipt at the destination. This is an example of reliable communication. In contrast, communications based on UDP packets are considered unreliable because they are not acknowledged. Because of this, less processing is required, and communications can occur more quickly. Still, it is ultimately up to the application to ensure that packets are exchanged reliably. The application typically decides which transport protocol (TCP or UDP) to use, based on its transmission requirements for speed versus reliability.

## IP Addresses

Each packet sent in the manner described in Figure 3-3 has source and destination information attached. The source and destination information is specified using Internet Protocol (IP) addresses. To avoid name space collisions, IP addresses are unique throughout the entire world of networks. An IP address is a 4-byte octet covering the range from 0.0.0.0 to 255.255.255.255. These addresses are divided into classes, shown in Table 3-1.

**Table 3-1** IP Address Classes

| Class | First Octet | Network Mask |
|-------|-------------|--------------|
| A | 001–126 | 255.0.0.0 |
| B | 128–191 | 255.255.0.0 |
| C | 192–223 | 255.255.255.0 |

Not all IP addresses in the designated range are available for use by normal computer networks. For example, the 127.x.x.x group of IP addresses is assigned for local machine information, and the 224.x.x.x group is assigned for multicasting.

### Subnets

For scalability and efficiency, the network layer is partitioned into subnets. Such partitioning enables the network layer to intelligently determine network routes and improve network performance by masking portions of IP addresses.

For example, let's say the client orange uses the IP address 129.152.221.41, and the server apple uses 129.152.221.1. Both machines are in the same class C subnet. The network layer applies the mask of 255.255.255.0 to incoming packets to determine whether they fall within the class C IP address range (using a true or false condition), and it does not attempt to route them outside the subnet unless necessary. This concept is described in Figure 3-4.

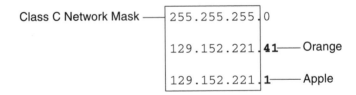

**Figure 3-4** Class C Subnet Network Mask

## LANs and WANs

A class C IP network can accommodate 255 IP addresses, making it suitable for a small office or a Local Area Network (LAN). A class B IP network provides 65,025 addresses, and it can be used in either a LAN or a Wide Area Network (WAN) that is distributed over many physical locations. A class A IP network provides 16,581,375 IP addresses, and it is typically used in a WAN.

### Network Devices

LANs and WANs may be comprised of network devices other than just clients, servers, and printers. For example, other network devices include repeaters, bridges, routers, and gateways. Each of these devices has specific networking functions:

- Repeater

    A repeater is a device that regenerates the data signal to extend the distance of the transmission. It is typically used to improve the signal to noise ratio in the physical link of the networking model discussed earlier.

- Bridge

    A bridge is a data link layer device that interconnects two networks of the same type. It examines address fields and selectively copies packets from one network segment to another bi-directionally.

- Router

    A router is a network layer component that forwards packets in the appropriate direction (to the next network hop) using a lookup table.

- Gateway

    A gateway is a device that primarily does protocol conversion between two different types of networks. It can be in the network, transport, or the application layer of the network model.

Typically, a LAN is connected using ethernet (10mb/sec or 100mb/sec); and a WAN is connected using a T1 (1.5mb/sec), DS1, or other leased lines such as ISDN.

### Internet Access

In an intranet, routing to the Internet is not performed inside of the firewall. Instead, Internet access is enabled using proxy servers and firewalls (see *Firewall and Proxy Services* on page 37 for more information).

## Network Analysis and Configuration Commands

In this section, we'll describe some commands that enable you to examine and network activity and configure TCP/IP settings. Unless otherwise noted, these commands are available in both the Solaris and Windows environments.

### *The* ifconfig *Command*

The ifconfig -a command in Solaris displays the current network configuration, as shown in Example 3-1.

**Example 3-1** ifconfig -a **Output**

```
# /usr/sbin/ifconfig -a
lo0: flags=849<UP,LOOPBACK,RUNNING,MULTICAST> mtu 8232
        inet 127.0.0.1 netmask ff000000
le0: flags=863<UP,BROADCAST,NOTRAILERS,RUNNING,MULTICAST> mtu 1500
        inet 129.152.221.41 netmask ffffff00 broadcast 129.152.221.255
        ether 8:0:20:81:1f:ba
```

You can also use the ifconfig command to temporarily change the network configuration, or to test a netmask, as shown below.

```
# /usr/sbin/ifconfig interface netmask mask options
```

In the following example, the ifconfig command is used to change the netmask:

```
# /usr/sbin/ifconfig ie0 host-name 255.255.255.0 broadcast + up
```

To permanently change the network mask, modify the /etc/inet/netmasks file. If you use a name service such as NIS, then modify the appropriate table.

To view the network configuration in Windows, select the Network icon from the control panel.The properties for the appropriate network interface and protocol are displayed, and you can make changes if necessary.

### *The* `ping` *and* `traceroute` *Commands*

The `ping` command sends a special Internet Control Message Protocol (ICMP) packet containing only header information to the destination address. The ICMP packet requests an acknowledgment of receipt, and it helps determine if the remote host is reachable using your current network configuration. The command is used as follows:

---

```
/usr/sbin/ping destination-host or IP-address
```

---

An example is provided below.

---

```
% /usr/sbin/ping host-name
host-name is alive
```

---

Optionally, you can obtain statistics using the `ping -s` command:

---

```
% /usr/sbin/ping -s host-name
PING host-name: 56 data bytes
64 bytes from host-name (IP-address): icmp_seq=0. time=1. ms
64 bytes from host-name (IP-address): icmp_seq=1. time=1. ms
64 bytes from host-name (IP-address): icmp_seq=2. time=0. ms
<Control-C>
```

---

In Windows, the `ping -n 100` command provides similar statistics.

In some instances, an intermediate router in the path to the destination may not forward the packet. This is when the `traceroute` command is useful (in Windows, the command is called `tracert`). Using the `traceroute` command, you can determine the route path for a packet starting from the source and ending at the destination. The intermediate routing hosts are displayed, and the time delays for the packet as it travels between each router are also shown.

The format for the command is shown below.

---

```
traceroute destination host or IP address
```

---

Output from the `traceroute` command is shown in Example 3-2.

**Example 3-2** `traceroute` **Output**

```
% traceroute host-name
traceroute to host-name (IP-address), 30 hops max, 40 byte packets
 1  apple (IP-address)    3 ms   2 ms   2 ms
 2  plum (IP-address)    107 ms   93 ms   94 ms
 3  potato (IP-address)   137 ms  144 ms  148 ms
 4  raisin (IP-address)   176 ms  162 ms  177 ms
 5  banana (IP-address)   185 ms  184 ms  178 ms
 6  peach (IP-address)    225 ms  188 ms  *
 7  host-name (IP-address)  199 ms   *   126 ms
```

### *The* `netstat -r` *Command*

At times, the routing tables stored in the local system may need to be modified or displayed while troubleshooting network problems. The `netstat -r` command displays the routing table of the current machine, subnet masks for various networks, gateway information needed to route packets, and so on.

Output from the `traceroute` command is shown in Example 3-3.

**Example 3-3** `netstat` **Output**

```
% netstat -r

Routing Table:
  Destination           Gateway              Flags  Ref   Use    Interface
  -------------------   -------------------  -----  ----- ------ -------
  localhost             localhost            UH     0     8692   lo0
  plum                  gate                 UGHD   0     0
  potato                gate                 UGHD   0     0
  raisin                gate                 UGHD   0     0
  banana                gate                 UGHD   0     0
  peach                 gate                 UGHD   0     0
  fruit-net1            gate                 U      3     9743   le0
  veggie-net2           gate-222             U      2     3132   le1
  224.0.0.0             gate                 U      3     0      le0
  default               wf-gate              UG     0     134366
```

### Network Configuration Files Used at Boot Time

In the Solaris environment, the following files are used to determine and configure the network interface at boot time.

- `/etc/nodename`

  Sets the machine's host name during the initial phase of the boot process.

- `/etc/inet/hosts`

  The file where the `localhost`, host name and IP address are stored.

- `/etc/inet/netmasks`

  The file used to set the netmask for local network interfaces.

- `/etc/hostname.`*interface*

  The file where the host names associated to each network interface are stored.

The `/etc/defaultrouter` file is used to populate the routing table with a default router and contains the router name. The host does not route packets itself, and instead forwards all packets that require routing to the default router.

## Summary

Communication across every intranet, and, in fact, the entire Internet is performed using the concepts and techniques described in this chapter. All intranet activities, from accessing a web site located in a remote country to printing a file to a network printer down the hall, make use of the networking layers and components we've described.

# CHAPTER

# 4

# Firewall and Proxy Services

Security is an important aspect in intranet design. Additionally, protecting computing resources and the information assets they store, and preventing unauthorized access to the intranet are among the most important intranet administration tasks. The Internet offers a wealth of information resources and communication opportunities to an intranet, but connecting to the Internet also presents a security challenge. Though enabling Internet access from within the intranet without compromising security is a balancing act, there are measures you can take to ensure the safety of your intranet. In this chapter, we'll look at strategies to safeguard an intranet.

## What is a Firewall?

The mechanism used to protect almost all intranets today is a *firewall*. A firewall is a generic term for hardware and/or software components that share the same goal of protecting the intranet from external attacks, while allowing Internet access from within the intranet. These components can include filters that block certain types of incoming transmissions, and gateways that provide specific relay services to compensate for the blocking effects of filters, as illustrated in Figure 4-1.

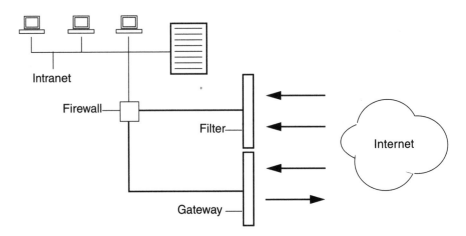

**Figure 4-1** Firewall Components

A firewall service can be implemented as a software solution, with a dual hosted setup and software configuration (for example, the TIS or Firewall-1), or it can be implemented purely in hardware, using packet filtering (for example, Sun's SPF-100). A packet filtering firewall drops packets based on packet destination or source (using IP addresses and/or ports). Addresses and ports that are safe to use are configured and installed on a router system that performs this filtering work.

The other type of firewall service is an application level firewall, which provides higher levels of security. The simplest form of an application level firewall is a computer with two network interfaces that does not allow packet routing between the interfaces. Other variations include two different computers—one connected to the Internet, and the other connected to the intranet. There is no direct packet level interaction between the two machines, but services are selectively connected between the two using special programs and a private network, as shown in Figure 4-2.

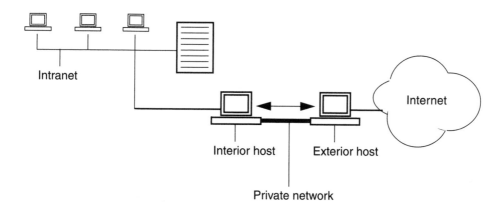

**Figure 4-2** Application Level Firewall

The only destination into the intranet for the exterior host is the interior host, and the interior host does not trust the exterior host.

The application level firewall is typical in a corporate intranet, and it allows only limited Internet services. For example, the exterior host receives e-mail messages destined for the intranet using SMTP. It then forwards the messages to the interior host for delivery. Services that originate in the intranet such as DNS services are not allowed to reach the Internet. Furthermore, no direct port connection from the Internet is allowed to any host inside the intranet. Only connections initiated on behalf of intranet hosts by the exterior machine can establish connections with the Internet, as shown in Figure 4-3.

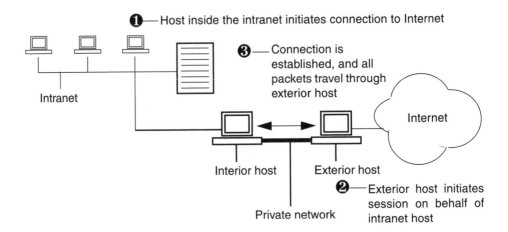

**Figure 4-3** Internet Access Using Application Level Firewall

These connections are TCP-based, and typically no UDP connections are permitted.

## Internet Access Services Provided by the Firewall

An application-level firewall configuration provides two types of services that enable Internet access, as described below. Since these services are implemented at the application level, the application source code may require modification before it will operate using the firewall.

- Any TCP connection using a firewall host

  In this scenario, a software application running on an intranet desktop wants to establish a connection to a host on the Internet. It establishes a connection to a special port on the firewall host, and passes the destination name (or IP address) and the port number to the firewall (using `connect(3N)`). The firewall then establishes the connection to the Internet machine, and transfers the connection to the intranet machine.

- A connection using the SOCKS protocol

  SOCKS is a special library of networking functions (such as connect, socket, and so on) that is linked into an application and replaces the normal networking functions. SOCKS enables applications to initiate connections to the Internet using a firewall.

# Proxy Services

Since both of the methods we just described require source code modification, it can be difficult to enable commercial software to access the Internet from within an intranet. To address this problem, many software packages provide a proxy function designed to operate within a firewall. For example, a web browser running on an intranet machine can use a proxy to access Internet resources. The proxy is a separate program that understands the application-specific protocol (in the Web example, HTTP), and it also understands how to communicate with the firewall. The proxies for popular protocols are freely available in source-code format so they can be customized for use within the intranet. Using a proxy, you don't have to worry about modifying the source code to a commercial Internet application such as Netscape Navigator, or the Real Audio player from Progressive Networks.

Let's look at effective ways to use proxies within an intranet. An HTTP proxy enables access to the Internet and intranet without compromising intranet security. Since a proxy sits between the client and the server, it can perform several useful functions.

## Caching

More and more intranet users are accessing the Web and visiting Internet sites. Each time a user visits a web site, several network connections are required to retrieve the data. Often, the same site is visited by a number of users. Large data files, such as images that seldom change, are retrieved repeatedly, with multiple users making redundant connections to the same web site. Ideally, only one visit to the remote web site should be required on behalf of all users, and this is where the caching proxy comes in. A proxy can cache frequently-accessed web pages to local disk. Subsequent requests for the same pages are handled by the caching proxy, without imposing unnecessary demands on the network. Users experience improved performance, and the network load is reduced. A single caching proxy can be used for a set of users in a subnet or domain.

Because it can quickly be filled with images and other data, the cache is set to a predetermined size. To avoid filling up the cache with outdated information that is no longer useful, the caching proxy uses a garbage collection feature that prunes the cache by removing data that is not likely to be requested again.

## Logging

A record of requested URLs is created using the logging feature of the proxy server. Though this information can provide useful statistics on the effectiveness of the proxy server cache, it also tracks the sites users are visiting, which can be seen as intrusive to some (if this is an issue for your organization, you can disable the logging feature). The log provides information about the effectiveness of the cache by recording the number of times the cache was referenced, as well as how many requests could not be completed because the information was not in the cache (the latter results in a network access by the proxy server to fetch the desired URL on behalf of the requestor).

### *Filtering*

Having control of the proxy server means having control over which web sites users can visit. Since access to sites outside the intranet is performed through the proxy server, you can block access to web sites based on their URLs.

### *DNS Lookups*

Since the proxy server accesses web data on behalf of the client, the client does not need to resolve the IP address of the server name in the URL using DNS—this work is done by the proxy server and the firewall. This saves time, since you need only configure the firewall to operate in the DNS name space of the Internet, and the client system can be configured to use intranet DNS services only.

## Limitations to Proxy Services

### *Caching Stale Documents*

A problem occurs if the data stored in the proxy server cache becomes out of date. A web browser relying on a caching proxy server might be given information that is no longer valid (this is also known as a "stale" document), and the user would not know the difference. To avoid distributing stale documents, the caching proxy server performs a cache consistency check, where it periodically fetches the last-modified time attribute from the HTTP server where the document originated. The caching proxy server compares this time stamp with that of the cached document, and discards the cached document if it is not current and fetches the new version from the HTTP server.

To avoid this problem entirely, some web sites use CGI scripts to render the HTML page on the fly each time the site is visited. Since CGI scripts are not cached by the proxy server, the proxy server is forced to fetch the web pages from the source each time the URL is requested.

### Secure Web Transactions

A web browser client in an intranet cannot perform secure transactions with a server that resides outside the firewall that uses either the SHTTP or SSL protocol. This is because the proxy server cannot cache this type of network traffic—doing so would introduce a security risk for any web transaction that requires a private and secure communications channel.

## Caching Proxies and Web Browsers

Because web browsers also cache recently used web data, let's talk about the relationship between a web browser cache and the proxy server cache. To accelerate web browsing activities, particularly when the user presses the Back or Forward buttons in the web browser, the browser caches data in memory and on disk. The browser searches for cached data in the following order:

* Main memory

  The web browser stores recently used data in its application memory space for the fastest access. This is a non-persistent storage area—it disappears when the user quits the Web browser.

* Disk

  Data is also cached to disk. If the disk is local, this reduces network access. Unlike the cache stored in memory, the disk is a persistent cache, and it can be used across multiple browsing sessions (on a per-user basis) and desktop reboots.

* Caching proxy

  If data is not found in either the memory or disk caches, the browser accesses the caching proxy server. This data is persistently stored on the server, and cached data is shared among multiple users, unlike the memory and disk caches, which are limited to a single web browser.

All caches can be bypassed if the user presses the Shift key and Reload button in the web browser. This instructs the browser to fetch data directly from the HTTP server, and ignore data stored in memory, disk, and proxy server caches.

## Cascading Proxies

A network topology with multiple caching proxy servers arranged in a hierarchy is called a cascading proxy configuration, or cascading proxies. In this configuration, multiple "slave" proxy servers share the same cache from a centralized "master" proxy server, as illustrated in Figure 4-4.

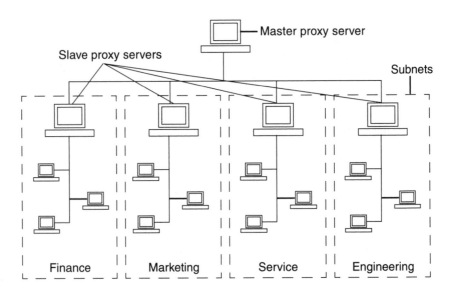

**Figure 4-4** Cascading Proxy Topology

This configuration is supported by the Netscape Proxy Server using the SOCKS protocol.

### *Avoiding Unnecessary Proxy Access*

Though you can efficiently distribute cached data using proxies, sometimes you're better off not using a proxy at all. For example, if a user requests data that is not cached from an HTTP server residing in the same subnet, the request requires three transactions—the first transaction occurs when the browser requests the data from the proxy, the second transaction is when the proxy requests the data from the server, and the last transaction is when the proxy returns the data to the browser.

Because the client browser and HTTP server reside on the same subnet, only a single transaction, not three, is required. This problem can be avoided by carefully configuring the web browser to not use a caching proxy for specified servers (usually in the same subnet).

### *Automatic Proxy Configuration*

To avoid problems with unnecessary proxy server access that can arise in a cascading proxy configuration, you can create a set of rules for web browsers that specify how to access the proxy servers. A web browser can be configured to automatically load a set of rules[1] that control proxy access based on desktop attributes such as the DNS domain, IP address, and so on. The rules can be used to specify which proxy servers the browser should bypass to contact an HTTP server directly, for example. They can also specify the location of proxy servers, and the order in which they should be accessed.

## Commercial Proxy Servers

Many commercial proxy servers are available from companies such as Netscape, and more recently, Microsoft. You can deploy proxy servers at the Internet gateway, or internally at remote offices or at major subnet levels. Typically, 100-300 desktops can be supported by a single proxy server.

For a departmental intranet, a proxy server deployed just behind the firewall facilitates access to the Internet and reduces response times and communications expense. A corporate intranet can deploy one per division such that marketing, sales, product development, human resources, and finance might all have their own subnetworks. By deploying proxy servers at each subnet, a company can reduce the traffic on the corporate backbone. If there are remote offices, a proxy server can provide a quick mechanism for replicating content, providing better company integration and increasing network performance over slow links. Proxy servers can also reduce the network bottleneck at the firewall points.

## Summary

A firewall service is essential if you intend to enable intranet users with direct access to the Internet. It helps to protect against unauthorized access to the intranet, and safeguards valuable intranet information assets. Still, you should ensure that a reliable backup policy is in place and working in case intranet security is breached. Caching proxy services provide you with a great way to distribute network loads, and they enable you to monitor and control web access from within your intranet. These services can also reduce network latencies in web browsing sessions, and they can improve web browser performance for many intranet users.

1.  To learn more about writing rules for automatic proxy configuration, visit http://www.netscape.com/comprod/server_central/product/proxy/index.htm /.

# CHAPTER

# 5

# Setting Up Remote Access Services

I n the chapters to come, we'll describe how to set up the intranet infrastructure and establish web services, file sharing, e-mail, and other intranet services. Since you are likely to encounter users outside of the physical boundaries of the LAN or WAN who need access to the intranet, let's visit this topic now. The types of employees who need remote access might include individuals who want to telecommute and work from home, users working at a remote site, or "roaming" employees who require access from just about anywhere.

To support this class of users, you can set up and configure remote access services. The technology that supports remote access has evolved over the years from simple terminal-based access using modems running at 1,200 bps to full blown IP connections using fast modems that support speeds up to 33,600 bps or greater. Integrated Services Digital Network (ISDN) technology has extended the bandwidth available for remote access to up to 128 Kbytes. Regardless of the hardware used to establish the connection, it's inevitable that the protocols used to enable remote access to intranet services will be based on the Internet Protocol. In this chapter, we'll look at a common IP-based protocol used for remote access, the Point-to-Point protocol, or PPP[1].

---

1.   For more information, visit http://www.internic.net/rfc/rfc1661.txt/.

## What is PPP?

PPP is the successor to an earlier protocol used to establish connections over a serial line, the Serial Line Internet Protocol, or SLIP. PPP is an evolving protocol, and it offers a number of advantages over SLIP, including:

- Improved performance

- Better reliability

- Enhanced security

- Better interoperability

PPP also supports the encapsulation of other network protocols, also known as "IP tunneling". This feature enables interoperability in environments that legacy protocols. In many ways, PPP is SLIP "done right." It is the de-facto standard used for Internet access by many modem-equipped users, and it does a great job of providing remote intranet access too. We won't cover how to configure remote access using SLIP, since the configuration is very similar to setting up PPP.

PPP is intended for use over slow serial links, such as dial-up connections established using modems on each end (it can also be used with faster connections, such as ISDN.) It enables you to extend the intranet to users at remote sites using public data networks maintained by common carriers, such as the phone company. Using PPP, users can run TCP/IP-based applications at remote locations over slower links. Since TCP/IP software is included with Windows and Solaris, PPP has evolved as the de-facto standard for remote connections.

## Remote Access Configuration Overview

A PPP connection is established between a server and a client. In a typical scenario, the remote user dials up the PPP server, and logs in using a special PPP account. This login automatically invokes a PPP program on the server, which initiates the handshake with the client and establishes the connection, as shown in Figure 5-1.

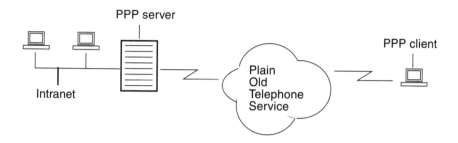

**Figure 5-1** Basic Remote Access Configuration

This configuration is suitable for a small intranet, but for a larger intranet, it's preferable to use a terminal server for all dial-in access, as shown in Figure 5-2.

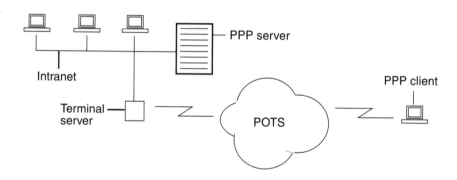

**Figure 5-2** Terminal Server Remote Access Configuration

With a terminal server, you can centralize outside access into the intranet to a single location that is easier to administer and safeguard. Most terminal servers support simple VT-100 type connections, which in turn can be used to establish PPP connections. A nice security feature that is offered by some vendors is a secure dial-back mechanism. With this feature, a remote user is authenticated twice—first, when the user logs into terminal server, and again when the terminal server calls backs to a predetermined phone number (usually, this is the remote location such as the user's home). No one is allowed to directly connect into the intranet without going through the dial-back process.

This might be an ideal configuration if all your users are accessing the intranet from a fixed remote site, but what about the user whose location changes all the time? For example, a salesperson may be traveling and require remote access from a hotel room, airport lobby, or just about anywhere. In this case, the secure dial-back is not useful, but there is an alternative using Data Encryption Standard technology. Using DES, the remote user can directly access the intranet without compromising security, as shown in Figure 5-3.

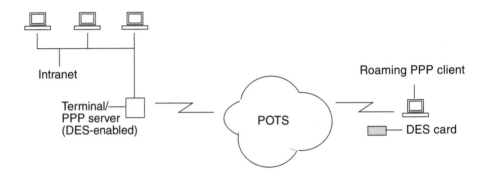

**Figure 5-3** Terminal Server Remote Access Configuration (DES)

The remote user is issued a DES digital token card. This battery-operated, credit-card sized device is used to generate encrypted passwords that are synchronized with a DES-enabled terminal server. A typical scenario works like this:

- The user dials in to the terminal server

- The terminal server generates a password key that has a finite lifetime

- The user turns on the DES card and enters the password key into the DES card, and the decrypted password is displayed

- The user types in the decrypted password

- The terminal server checks the password against its decrypted password, and allows access if there is a match, and denies access if there is a mismatch

It is difficult for anyone who wants to gain unauthorized access to the intranet to break in using a password that was obtained illicitly, because the passwords are constantly changing.

If the terminal server is capable of providing PPP services, this is the ideal configuration. The terminal server can dynamically allocate an IP address to a roaming client from a pool of IP addresses reserved for this purpose. Most of the administration and configuration required to provide remote access services (beside the remote client configuration) is performed in a centralized, secure manner.

To help you understand what is involved in establishing PPP services, we'll look at how to set up a basic remote access configuration. We'll assume there is a terminal server in place, but we won't go into the specifics of how to configure it since this varies. We'll show how to configure a PPP server running Solaris, and then we'll configure a Windows 95 PPP client to connect to the server. This will give you an overview of how to configure PPP for both environments. It also reflects a heterogenous environment using industry standard protocols.

## Setting Up PPP Services on a Solaris Server

To set up PPP services on a Solaris server, you'll first need to obtain preliminary network configuration information, then use this information to run a script designed to easily set up the PPP server.

### Preliminary Network Information

You will need the following information to set up PPP services for each remote client.

• PPP client host name and IP address

  The remote client accesses intranet services as if it was locally attached to the LAN. Just like a desktop on the LAN, it must be configured with TCP/IP services, and the host name and IP address is required for the PPP configuration.

• PPP login

  This is the special user login that invokes PPP services. The PPP login is usually the existing user login prepended with a P character, as in *Puser*.

• PPP server host name

  You should try to centralize PPP services on a single server, if possible. This enables you to manage PPP services more effectively, since configuration information such as PPP logins are stored in a centralized manner.

### PPP Setup Script

To help you set up PPP services on the server, the script shown in Example 5-1 is provided. This script requires the Solaris 2.5.*x* operating environment (if your PPP server is running an earlier version of Solaris such as Solaris 2.4, you must install the SUNWpppk, SUNWapppr, and SUNWapppu packages).

To use this script, you must replace the following values:

- PPPHOST

  This is the host name for the remote PPP client.

- IP

  This is the IP address assigned to the remote PPP client.

- USER

  This is the special user login that invokes PPP services. The PPP login is usually the existing user login prepended with a P character, as in P*user*.

- HOST

  This is the host name for the PPP server.

**Example 5-1** `pppsetup.sh` **Solaris PPP Service Set Up Script**

```
#!/bin/sh
# replace these fields
PPPHOST=ppp-client
IP=xxx.xxx.xxx.xxx
USER=Puser
HOST=ppp-server

grep -s $PPPHOST $T/etc/hosts || {
   echo ***adding $PPPHOST to /etc/hosts
   echo "$IP  $PPPHOST" >> $T/etc/hosts
}

test -f $T/etc/defaultrouter && {
   rm -f $T/etc/defaultrouter
}

test -f $T/etc/gateways || {
   echo ***creating /etc/gateways
   echo "norip ipdptp0" > $T/etc/gateways
}

grep -s $USER $T/etc/asppp.cf >/dev/null 2>&1 || {
   echo "***Install PPP configuration"
cat >> $T/etc/asppp.cf <<EOF_P
debug_level 6     # 9 is good for debugging  errors
ifconfig ipdptp0 plumb $HOST $PPPHOST netmask + down

defaults
              interface         ipdptp*
        inactivity_timeout 90000
        ipcp_async_map 0
        lcp_mru 256

path
              peer_system_name $USER
              peer_ip_address $PPPHOST
EOF_P
}
```

```
grep -s $USER $T/etc/passwd >/dev/null 2>&1 || {
cat >> $T/etc/passwd <<EOF_PA
${USER}:x:101:1:${USER} PPP account:/:/usr/sbin/aspppls
EOF_PA
cat >> $T/etc/shadow <<EOF_SH
${USER}::6445::::::
EOF_SH
echo "Created account for $USER on $HOST"
echo "Set password on first login"
}

echo "Reboot $HOST to start PPP services"
```

## Setting Up PPP for a Windows 95 Client

The remote client we'll configure is a desktop running Windows 95. This might be a desktop located at the user's home, or it could be located at a remote office in the field. Regardless, the user needs to access the intranet services such as web services and e-mail. We'll walk you through the configuration steps needed to set up the remote client with PPP services.

Following is an overview of the tasks required to set up PPP on the remote client.

- Obtain preliminary network configuration information

- Verify software installation and configurations

- Configure the network identity

- Configure TCP/IP software

- Create the Dial-Up connection (dial-up icon)

### Preliminary Network Information

Before you begin setting up PPP services, you should have the following network information handy, as you will be prompted for this information during the setup process.

- IP Address

    This is the IP address assigned to your remote Windows 95 client.

- Subnet Mask

    This is the netmask used for your IP subnet class in decimal dot notation. Usually, this value is 255.255.255.0.

- NIS host name

  This is the host name assigned to your remote Windows 95 client as it appears in the NIS.

- DNS domain name

  This is the fully qualified domain name your Windows 95 client uses for host name resolution.

- DNS server IP address(es)

  This is the primary DNS server IP address in decimal dot notation. If a secondary DNS is available, its IP address should be noted as well.

- Subnet router IP address

  This is the router system IP address that receives and forwards IP packets for the subnet in which your Windows 95 client is a member.

### *PPP Configuration*

1.  **Verify that the Dial-Up Networking software is installed.**
    Choose Control Panel ➤ Add/Remove Programs ➤Windows Setup
    Communications ➤ Details. The Dial-Up networking control panel is
    displayed.

If necessary, install the Dial-Up Networking component.

**2.** **Verify that the Dial-Up Adapter is configured.**

Choose Control Panel ➤ Network ➤ Configuration. The Dial-Up Adapter control panel is displayed.

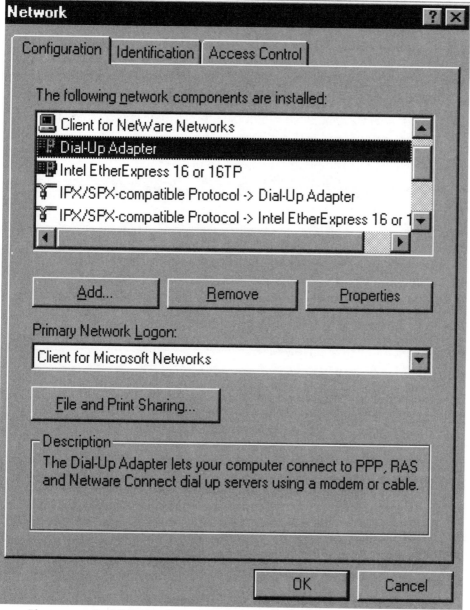

If necessary, add the Dial-Up Adapter configuration.

**3.**   **Verify that the TCP / IP Dial-Up Adapter is configured.**

An example is shown below.

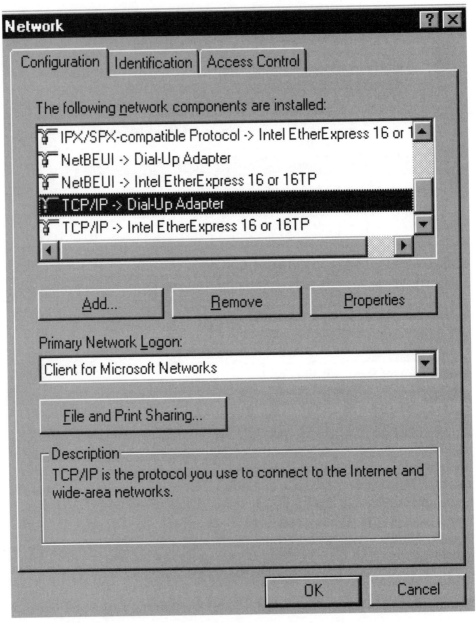

If necessary, add the TCP/IP Dial-Up Adapter configuration.

4.  **Select the Identification tab in the Network window.**
    The Identification window is displayed.

5.  **Enter the name of your PC and set the Workgroup name in the Identification window.**
    If you are using the NIS in the intranet, enter the PC name as it is stored in NIS. An example is shown below.

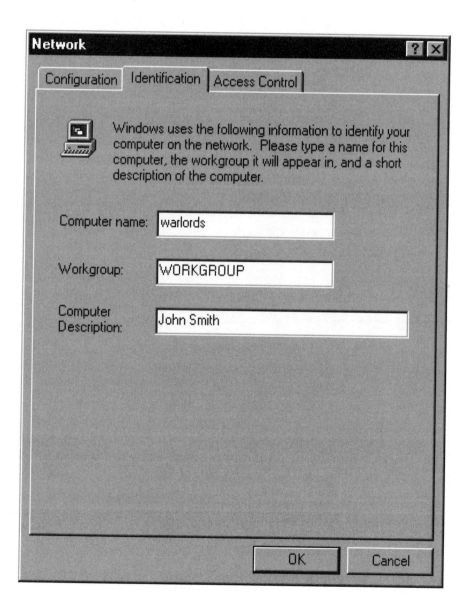

6.  **Choose the Configuration tab in the Network window.**
    The Configuration window is displayed.

7.  **Double-click the TCP / IP ➤ Dial-Up Adapter network component.**
    The TCP/IP Properties window is displayed. We'll enter TCP/IP settings such as the client IP address and the DNS server information here.

    - **IP Address**
      Enter the IP address assigned to your PC, and the subnet mask (usually 255.255.255.0).

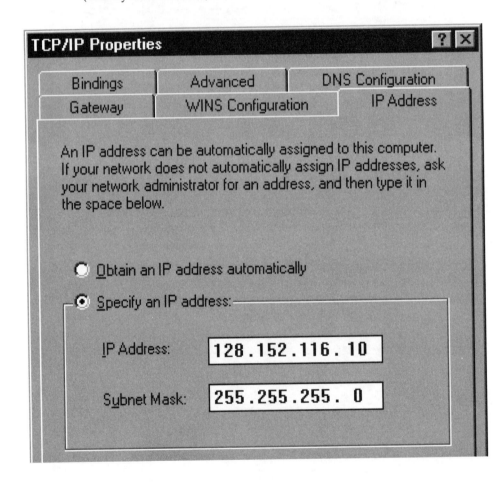

- **DNS Configuration**

    Click on the DNS Configuration tab in the TCP/IP Properties window.
    The DNS Configuration window is displayed.

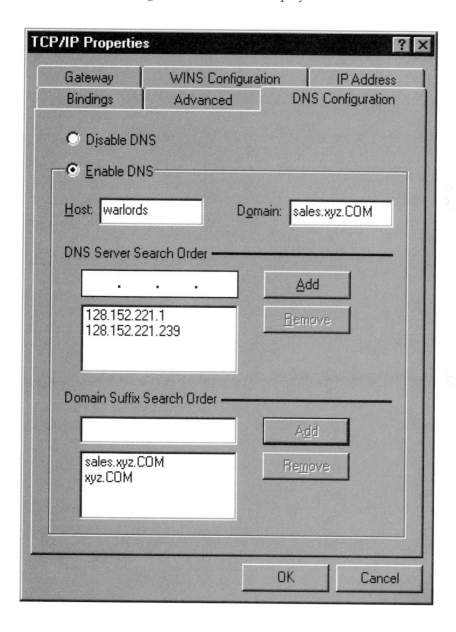

Enter your PC hostname in the Host dialog. The Domain should be your fully qualified DNS domain name, such as sales.xyz.COM. The DNS server search order should be in the decimal dot notation format (for example, xxx.xxx.xxx.xxx). The Domain Suffix Search Order should be sales.xyz.COM and xyz.COM.

- **WINS Configuration**

  Click on the WINS Configuration tab in the TCP/IP Properties window. The WINS Configuration window is displayed.

  This setting is not used, and should be disabled.

- **Advanced**

  Click on the Advanced tab in the TCP/IP Properties window. The Advanced window is displayed. This setting is not used, and should be empty (or select None).

- **Gateway**

    Click on the Gateway tab in the TCP/IP Properties window. The Gateway window is displayed.

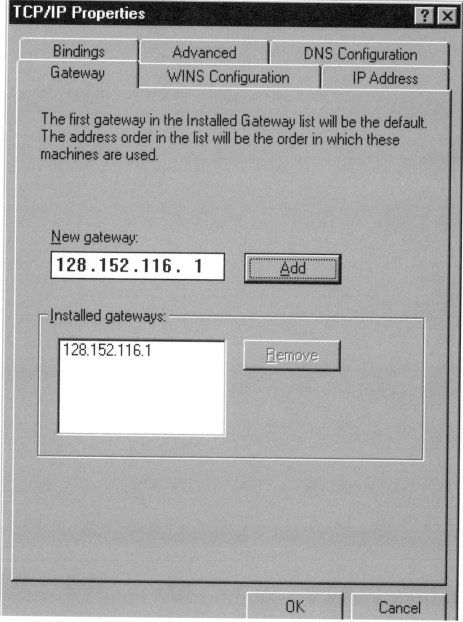

Enter the IP address of the subnet router.

- **Bindings**

  Click on the Bindings tab in the TCP/IP Properties window. The Bindings window is displayed. The Bindings window should indicate that the **Client for Microsoft Networks** and **File and Printer Sharing for Microsoft Networks** components will use PPP.

8. **Create the Dial-Up connection icon.**
   Choose My Computer ➤ Dial-Up Networking ➤Make New Connection. The Make New Connection window is displayed.

9. **Select the modem attached to your system. If necessary, click Configure to configure the modem attached to the system.**

10. **Set the baud rate and connection settings that are appropriate for your modem.**

    An example is shown below.

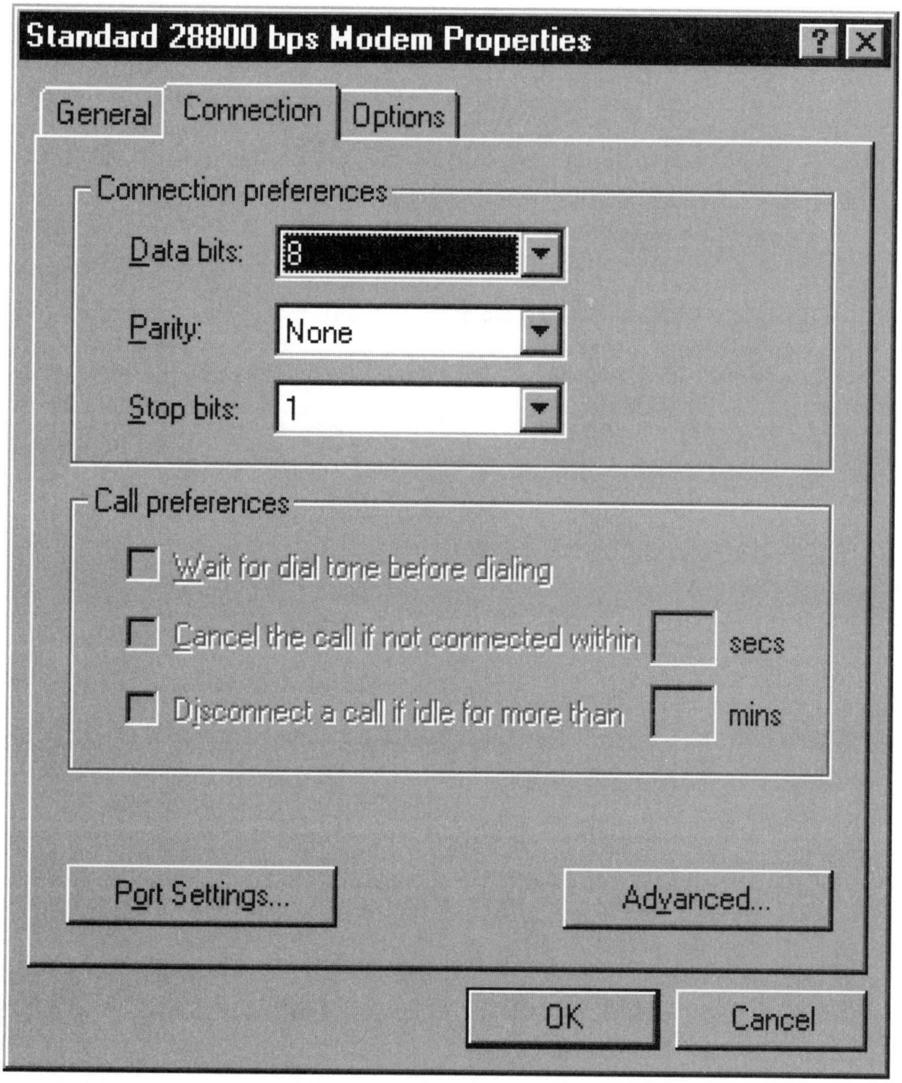

If your connection uses a dial-back mechanism, perform the following configuration steps.

**11.** **Select the Properties ➤ Configure ➤ Options menu item for the dial-up icon.**

The Modem Properties window is displayed.

**12.** **Check the connection control box to bring up a terminal window.**
An example is shown below.

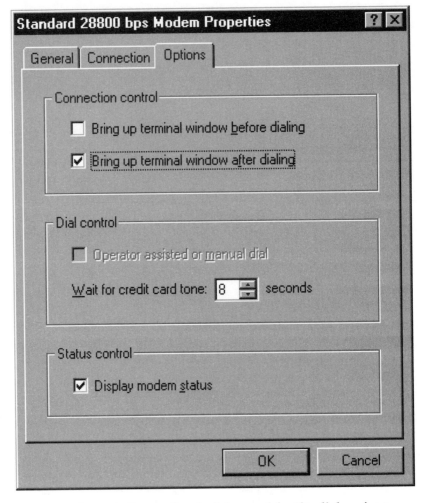

**13.** **Select Configure ➤Connection ➤ Advanced for the dial-up icon.**
The Connection window is displayed.

**14.** Add the string S0=1&C0 to the Extra Settings field so that dial-back is enabled and carrier detect is set to ON.

An example is shown below.

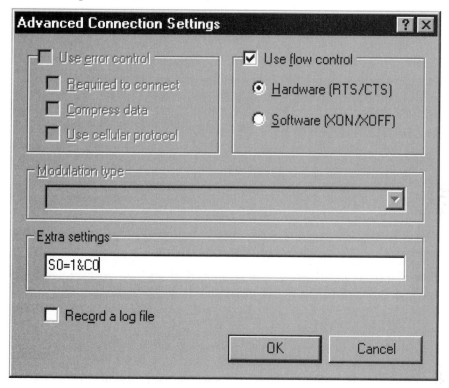

### Establishing the PPP Connection

Now you're ready to establish a PPP connection from the remote client to the server.

**1.** Start the dial-up process.

Click on the Dial-Up icon representing the connection you added earlier.

**2.** Type in your UNIX login and password.

If you are using a dial-back configuration, wait for the dial-back and type in the second login and password.

**3.** The terminal server login prompt appears.

**4.** Type in your PPP server name.

**5.** Type in your PPP user account login name, and use the same UNIX password.

6.  **Wait for few seconds for PPP process to start, and then press the F7 key to continue.**
    The PPP connection is established.

### Automating the PPP Connection Procedure

After successfully establishing your PPP connection to the intranet, you can automate the PPP connection procedure. You can use dscript[2] or RoboDUN[3] to script responses to prompts for logins, passwords, and other information, and you'll then be able to connect with a single mouse-click.

## Remote File Sharing and Printing

Once you have established your PPP connection to the intranet, you can access files using Windows 95 applications such as Microsoft Explorer. If a LAN Manager server such as Samba is available, you can also use the Microsoft Network Neighborhood to browse other Windows desktops in the LAN as well. For more information, see *Setting Up File Sharing and Printing Services* on page 143.

### Printer Access Using the Add Printer Wizard

You can also print directly from your remote client to an intranet printer. To do this you need to create a printer configuration on your Windows 95 desktop.

1.  **Select My Computer ➤ Printers ➤ Add Printer.**
    The Add Printer Wizard window is displayed.

2.  **Use the Add Printer Wizard to add a network printer.**
    You should be able to browse the network using the Add Printer Wizard and select an intranet printer such as \\server\printer-name.

## Optimizing Remote Access

### Using Winsock-Based Applications over PPP

Now that you have established a PPP connection to the intranet, your remote Windows 95 client is part of the LAN. It uses an IP address, and is capable of sending and receiving IP packets. You can use any Winsock-based TCP/IP applications[4] from your remote client, and send IP packets using the PPP connection established over the serial line.

---

2.  For more information, visit
    http://www.windows95.com/connect/dscript.html/.
3.  For more information, visit http://www.32bit.com/.
4.  To find more Winsock-based applications, visit ftp://ftp.cdrom.com/ or
    http://www.charm.net/.

Windows 95 provides Telnet, an application used to access remote computers using a terminal interface, and Internet Explorer, a web browser.

### Using Multiple TCP/IP Configurations

On occasion, the remote client may need to establish a PPP connect to locations other than the intranet, such as an Internet Service Provider (ISP). The DNS information for an ISP is different from the intranet, and you are required to change the TCP/IP settings each time you want to connect. Instead of manually changing the TCP/IP settings, a better alternative is to use a utility like netswitcher[5]. Netswitcher saves TCP/IP settings on a per-connection basis and restores them in the system registry upon demand. It enables you to quickly change TCP/IP settings without having to re-enter the DNS and IP addresses yourself. Netswitcher works for both Dial-Up connections and for direct, Ethernet-based connections.

### Using X-based Applications Remotely

Besides using Winsock-based applications over the PPP connection, you can also use applications based on the X-Windows protocol. Typically, these are applications that run in the X-Windows environment, such as `mailtool`, `calendar manager`, and possibly other X-Windows based applications you may have developed in-house.

To run X-Windows based applications remotely, you need a TCP/IP-based X Windows server that is capable of using Microsoft's Winsock. An example is SunSoft's PC-X[6] product. This X-Windows server is designed for Windows 95 and is installed and runs on the remote Windows 95 client, and it enables you to run X-Window clients either remotely or locally on your Windows 95 PC. PC-X is a 32 bit, Winsock compliant X11R6-based commercial X-Windows server product. With this software, you can create desktop icons pointing to an X-Windows application (for example, `xterm` and `mailtool`) and launch them by simply double-clicking an icon on your desktop.

---

5.  To obtain this utility, visit http://www.bysnet.com/netsw.html/.
6.  For more information, visit http://www.sun.com/sunsoft/solstice/Networking-products/PC-X.html/.

### *Other Useful Windows 95 Applications*

- Solstice PC-CacheFS

Solstice PC-CacheFS[7] is an innovative product for Windows 95 that can significantly improve your file data retrieval performance using disk-based persistent caching technology. Using PC-CacheFS, you can significantly increase the performance of your remote PPP connection.

## Summary

Remote access services extend the boundaries of an intranet and accommodate users who can't be at the office but still require intranet access to perform their jobs. Remote access can also improve the quality of life for many employees by enabling them to be productive from their homes or from remote sites. In large cities where commuting is a weary and time-consuming chore, telecommuting is an attractive and desirable alternative for many employees. For those employees who travel frequently, remote access is often a necessity because it links them to the information they need to obtain quotes using e-mail, enter customer orders using a web browser, and perform other important business functions tied to the services provided by an intranet.

7.   For more information, visit http://www.sun.com/sunsoft/solstice/em-products/system/pccache/PCCacheFS.html/. A demo is available.

# Building the Services Infrastructure

**PART THREE**

# CHAPTER

# 6

# Server-Centric Computing

In the chapters to come, we'll look at how to exploit the capabilities of an intranet by providing a rich set of services to every client in the network. In this chapter, we'll introduce a management technique that promotes efficiency, cost-effectiveness, and centralized administration. This style of computing is called *server-centric* computing.

## What is Server-Centric Computing?

Simply put, server-centric computing attempts to move as much data as possible off desktop computers and onto server systems, where it can be more easily managed. Following are examples of data that should be centralized:

- User files
- Configuration information
- Software applications

Clients access the data stored on servers using a network service. Examples of network services are shown in Table 6-1.

**Table 6-1** Intranet Information Types and Servers

| The Data Type ... | Is Hosted on the Server Type ... | Using This Network Service |
|---|---|---|
| User files | Home directory server | NFS |
| Login and password | Name service server | NIS/NIS+ |
| Application software | File server | NFS |
| Web pages | Web server | HTTPD |

In later chapters, we'll describe how to set up these and other network services using server-centric techniques.

### *Benefits*

Centralizing data on servers greatly reduces the scope of the administrative effort that is needed to provide reliable access to information. For example, by consolidating home directories onto a single home directory server, the task of backing up user files is greatly simplified. Users are not required to back up or restore the files since they do not reside on the local hard disk. Using a file sharing service, they utilize the network to access files stored on a file server. Access to the data occurs transparently and seamlessly — users read and write the files as if they were stored locally.

## The Thin Client

When data is no longer tied to an individual desktop computer, the desktop becomes insignificant. Since the information resources are persistently stored on servers that are carefully maintained, the desktop becomes a tool for accessing and creating information, but not for storing it. This relieves the administrative burden of having to treat desktop computers and other clients in the network as unique entities. Instead, they can be considered as *thin clients* —machines that can be easily replaced because they are just network devices that rely on the network and network services to do work. Note that thin clients are not "dumb" computing devices. They can still use the powerful processors and advanced windowing environments that users crave. The difference is that they are managed more effectively.

## Network Services

As you may have surmised, a server-centric computing model relies heavily on the network to enable clients with access to intranet resources. The TCP/IP network used in an intranet is ideal, since it allows the highest degree of heterogeneity among client and server platforms and operating environments. A myriad number of clients that are TCP/IP-capable can tap into the array of available services.

## Summary

Server-centric computing is a service-oriented management philosophy for an intranet. This model is based on the premise that information is better managed if it is centralized, and that network services are the key to providing access to information. With server-centric computing, the following goals are achieved:

- Data is controlled and managed on the network

- There is a lower cost of ownership for the enterprise

- Management efforts are focused on providing services to clients, and not managing the clients

- Barriers to the creation and sharing of information are eliminated

# CHAPTER

# 7

# Managing
# Operating
# System
# Software

In upcoming chapters, we'll examine the tasks required to set up your intranet, and establish important intranet services, such as e-mail, web services, and so on. An important prerequisite administration task is setting up the resources that make up the intranet infrastructure. These resources include the desktop computers and server systems in the intranet, for example. This normally starts with setting up the hardware, and it is followed by software installation, configuration, and administration tasks. Unfortunately, these tasks can be time-consuming and expensive. Setting up or re-installing an intranet resource for proper operation adds significantly to its cost of ownership. When taken as a whole, the cost of managing intranet resources such as desktops and servers can exceed the initial cost of the assets themselves.

Fortunately, there are software services available to help reduce the cost of installing and configuring intranet resources. Solaris Jumpstart[1] provides automatic operating system (OS) installation and configuration for Solaris desktops and servers in a non-interactive, "hands-off" manner. Windows provides a similar capability, using a machine profile with the setup program to perform non-interactive installation of the operating system. Installing the OS in this manner offers several advantages:

• It enables consistent OS configurations

1. The definitive JumpStart guide is *Automating Solaris Installations*, by Paul Anthony Kasper and Alan L. McClellan, 1995, SunSoft Press. ISBN: 0-13-312505-X

- Users can reinstall the OS, without requiring assistance from the administrator

- The administrator can manage the OS installation profile in a centralized manner

In this chapter, we'll look at how to use each of these technologies to facilitate operating system installation and configuration for both Solaris and Windows.

## Establishing OS Installation Requirements

Before we delve into the details of how to automate OS installation, let's first consider key concepts that can help you better plan and organize OS installation activities.

### User Profiles

Within an intranet, you will probably find that desktop users fall into different categories or *classes*. For example, a user in the finance department has hardware and software requirements that are similar to most other users in finance. The finance user has needs that differ from other types of users—the finance user doesn't need compiler software installed on the desktop, but for an engineering user, this is absolutely essential.

Besides application software, an area where users share similarities is in the configuration of the computer system used, such as CPU type and speed, installed memory size, hard disk size, and so on. This is an important factor to consider when upgrading the OS, for example, since some desktop computers may not have adequate disk space to perform a full installation, or they may not be compatible with a specific version of the OS.

You can use similarities shared by users to your advantage by standardizing on a configuration or *profile* for a particular type of user. These concepts are used by the JumpStart software to automate OS installation and upgrades, so it helps to create a list of desktop profiles and specify the requirements for each type of user beforehand.

### OS Customization

Solaris, Windows, and other OS environments provide you with the capability to customize the system software during the installation process (remember, we're discussing operating system software installation here, and not third-party application software installation, which is described in *Managing Software* on page 99). The problem with performing a custom installation is that it can be a time-consuming and error-prone process that inhibits standardization.

To avoid these problems, you can determine how the OS must be customized for a given user profile, and use these parameters to enable automated custom installation (in Solaris, this is called custom JumpStart).

### Post-Installation OS Configuration

A common activity is to configure the OS software after it is installed. For example, a newly-installed system may require the following:

- IP address assignment
- DNS configuration
- File sharing setup
- Services setup

Like customizing the OS, these post-installation activities can be error-prone, and they are ideal candidates for automation. Fortunately, you can specify post-installation instructions using `finish` scripts in the JumpStart software. Similarly, post-installation is supported in Windows by adding custom sections to `.inf` files.

## Solaris JumpStart

Solaris OS installation using JumpStart is done by setting up an OS server that contains the OS distribution. This OS distribution is mounted using NFS by the install clients for installation. The install clients boot from the network and bootstrap a mini-OS that is transferred from a boot server. This mini-OS has adequate intelligence to perform the access to the OS server using NFS. In JumpStart, Solaris provides a mechanism to install the operating system software in an intranet based on a profile. The desktop profile is used by JumpStart to automatically perform the following types of activities:

- Format disks
- Assign partitions
- Create file systems
- Install selected software

All of these activities are done in a "hands-off" manner. To install or upgrade the OS, a desktop user simply boots the install client, and the JumpStart software takes over. JumpStart uses the network, configuration files, and OS installation services to completely install, customize, and configure the system without any intervention. This is another example of centralizing administration activities in the intranet using a server-centric computing model.

### JumpStart Components

To use JumpStart, you must first set up the services that are required for automatic, network-based OS installation. After these services are set up, it is very easy to install and upgrade any Solaris desktop or server in the intranet. These are the server types required for network OS installation.

- **Install/Boot server**—a server with an image of the Solaris CD distribution and booting support for install clients. A single server can perform both functions, but if the install client is on a separate subnet, a separate boot server is required on that subnet.

- **Profile server**—a server with essential custom JumpStart configuration files.

- **NIS server**—a server with an NIS or NIS+ distributed name service database, providing default system configuration information for install clients.

Once these servers are available, you create profiles containing installation instructions for a specific system or for a class of systems. JumpStart uses this information to install the OS software. In this section, we'll describe how to set up the JumpStart software to support network-based OS installation, as it supports the server-centric computing model.

### JumpStart Overview

Following is an overview of the major tasks required to set up the JumpStart software.

- Set up the install/boot server

- Set up the profile server

- Enable the install client

### Setting Up the Install / Boot Server

JumpStart uses the Solaris OS distribution CD for installation purposes. You can insert the CD into a locally-attached CD-ROM on the install client, but it is preferable to copy the CD image to an NFS server so that it can be used across the network by all clients. The directory is then made available as a read-only file system on the server (the CD can also be shared without copying it to the local file system, but installation performance suffers).

1.  **Log into the server as root.**

2.  **Insert the Solaris OS distribution CD into the CD-ROM drive.**

**3.**   **Copy the CD image to the server.**

```
# volcheck
# cd /cdrom/cdrom/s0
# ./setup_install_server /export/os-dist
```

This command copies the Solaris OS distribution CD image to the
/export/osdist directory, and exports it on a read-only basis using
NFS.

### Setting Up the Profile Server

Next, we'll create the desktop profile used to specify the installation parameters.
Similar to the install server, this information is shared using NFS from a read-only
directory on a server. The profile server can be a different server than the install
server, but for the sake of simplicity, we'll use just a single server. The only
restriction is that the directory containing the desktop profiles on the profile
server must be exported to the install clients.

**1.**   **Log into the server as root.**

**2.**   **Create the directory to store the profiles.**

```
# mkdir /export/dtprof
```

**3.**   **Share the directory.**

```
# share -F nfs -o ro /export/dtprof
```

**4.**   **Restart the NFS server processes.**

```
# /etc/init.d/nfs.server stop
# /etc/init.d/nfs.server start
```

### Creating the JumpStart Profile

A JumpStart profile is a set of instructions that describes how the OS is to be
installed, and it consists of the following:

- Disk partition information
- List of software packages to be installed

- Commands to be executed after the installation (but before the reboot) of the desktop (also known as a `finish` script)

The JumpStart profile can also contain a set of commands called a `begin` script to be executed prior to the installation of the OS. You can use a begin script to back up files from the system before it is installed, for example.

### Basic JumpStart Profile

Example 7-1 shows the basic JumpStart profile we'll use for an install client.

**Example 7-1** `dtprof` **Basic JumpStart Profile**

```
❶ install_type   initial_install
❷ system_type    standalone
❸ partitioning explicit
❹ filesys c0t3d0s0 50    /
   filesys c0t3d0s1 128   swap
   filesys c0t3d0s6 450   /usr
   filesys c0t3d0s5 free  /opt
❺ cluster SUNWCall
```

An explanation of the entries in the basic JumpStart profile is provided below.

❶  The OS is installed and replaces any previously-installed version (not an upgrade).

❷  A standalone desktop system is installed.

❸  The partition parameters (such as the partition layout) are specified within the profile (not the default).

❹  This line indicates the disk to format (`c0t3d0`), and the location, size, and mount point for each partition (the remaining disk space is placed in the "free" partition, `/opt`).

❺  This instructs JumpStart to install the Solaris software cluster containing the entire OS distribution (`SUNWCall`) onto the desktop.

### Custom JumpStart Profile

In Example 7-2, we show how the profile can be used to specify custom partitioning and software selection.

**Example 7-2** `dtprof2` **Custom JumpStart Profile**

```
install_type   initial_install
system_type    standalone
partitioning explicit
```

**Example 7-2** `dtprof2` **Custom JumpStart Profile** **(Continued)**

```
❶ filesys c0t3d0s0 free /
  filesys c0t3d0s1 64  swap
  filesys c0t3d0s6 350  /usr
❷ filesys c0t3d0s7 existing /other  preserve
❸ cluster SUNWCprog
❹ package SUNWabe delete
```

An explanation of the entries in the custom JumpStart profile is provided below.

❶  This indicates the disk to format (`c0t3d0`), and the location, size, and mount point for each partition (the remaining disk space is placed in the "free" partition, `/`).

❷  The disk partition `/other` is preserved (the contents of the partition are untouched during the installation).

❸  This instructs JumpStart to install the Solaris Programmer's software cluster (`SUNWCprog`) onto the desktop.

❹  The AnswerBook (`SUNWabe`) package in the specified cluster is not installed.

### *Additional JumpStart Profile Parameters*

You can specify a number of other installation instructions in the JumpStart profile. For example, you can use Jumpstart to format and partition an install client with more than one disk (for example, `d0` and `d1`) and on more than one SCSI target (for example, `t3` and `t1`), as shown in this example.

```
filesys c0t3d1s1 64  swap
filesys c0t3d0s6 350  /usr
filesys c0t1d0s2 350  /local
```

An install client can also be a server that supports multiple platforms (for example, SPARC and x86) and platform groups (for example, Sun4m and Sun4c). In the following example, a Solaris server is installed with the software packages necessary to support clients that use the Sun4u (Ultra) platform group.

```
system_type server
client_arch sun4u
partitioning explicit
```

### Enabling the Install Client

After creating the desktop profile, you need to enable the JumpStart server with support for the install client.

```
# cd /export/osdist
# ./add_install_client profile-server:/export/dtprof desktop1 sun4m
```

In this example, sun4m specifies the platform type for the install client desktop1 (the platform can be obtained using the uname  -m command), and *profile-server* is the NFS server that shares the JumpStart profiles (see *Setting Up the Profile Server* on page 81).

In Example 7-1, we created the basic JumpStart profile for the install client, desktop1. Now, we need to verify that this profile is valid. In the directory we designated as the repository for JumpStart profiles, we'll modify the rules file (the rules file is a look-up table consisting of one or more rules that define how install clients are installed, based on their system attributes). We'll edit the /export/dtprofile/rules file and add the following entry.

```
hostname desktop1  -  desktop1.prof  -
```

Next, we'll create a Makefile to help us manage the JumpStart profile. This file is stored in the /export/dtprofile directory.

```
OSDIR=/net/jserver/export/osdist

rules.ok: rules
        $(OSDIR)/auto_install_sample/check -p $(OSDIR)
```

Now, we'll verify the JumpStart profile we specified in the rules file using the make command.

```
# cd /export/dtprofile
# /usr/ccs/bin/make
```

The make command executes the instructions in the `Makefile`, which in turn creates a `rules.ok` file that is used by JumpStart to map install client host names to install profiles. Each time you create a new profile for an install client, you must add an entry to the `rules` file and use the `make` command to update the `rules.ok` file.

### Booting the Install Client

Now the JumpStart server is completely enabled with OS installation support for the install client `desktop1`. The JumpStart profile that specifies disk partitioning parameters and the software configuration for `desktop1` is obtained from the JumpStart server.

To start the installation, we enter into the Open Boot prom mode. To enter this mode, type the L1 and A simultaneously. At the `ok` prompt, issue the following boot command on `desktop1`.

```
ok boot net - install
```

The install client boots from the network similar to the diskless client, using the services enabled for it on the JumpStart server. The instructions in the JumpStart profile are used to install the OS. After the installation is completed, the install client reboots itself, all in a hands-off manner. If additional information is needed to perform installation that JumpStart can't obtain from the network (such as the local and time zone), you will be prompted to supply it.

### Supporting Additional Install Clients

You can set up JumpStart profiles for all Solaris systems and store them in the same directory. For example, to support the install client `desktop2`, you can create the JumpStart profile `desktop2.prof` and store it in the shared NFS directory `/export/dtprofile`. The corresponding entry in the `/export/dtprofile/rules` file appears as follows.

```
hostname desktop2 - desktop2.prof -
```

In case a system does not have a matching profile, it can still be installed by using a catch-all default profile, as shown below.

---

```
any          -           -  default.prof  -
```

---

The advantage to setting up support for all Solaris systems in the intranet is that you can save time by easily reinstalling and upgrading the OS using JumpStart, as opposed to having to perform these tasks by hand.

## Windows Setup

Similar to Solaris JumpStart, Windows systems can be installed in an automated manner using a machine profile and the `setup` installation program. Unlike Solaris install clients that boot over the network, Windows systems need to be boot strapped manually. A boot floppy with network card drivers can be used to boot the Windows system into DOS mode and establish the network connections to the OS distribution server and profiles. In this section, we'll look at how to set up automated installation for Windows 95 (the configuration steps are similar for Windows NT, but the keywords used in the machine profile differ).

### The `setup` *Installation Program*

The Windows operating system is installed using the `setup` program. Though `setup` is normally run in interactive mode, you can supply it with an argument that specifies a file with directives for installing and configuring the Windows desktop. The input file is a machine profile for the `setup` program, and it contains pre-defined keywords and values which are used by `setup` as answers to the questions normally asked during a manual, interactive installation.

## The Windows Machine Profile

The keywords recognized by `setup` are grouped into areas which correspond to different stages of the installation.

### Setup

The `Setup` area of a machine profile file is shown in Example 7-3, and it is used to perform a quick "Express"-style installation of the Windows OS.

**Example 7-3** `setup` Express Machine Profile

```
  [Setup]
  Express=1
❶ InstallDir="C:\WIN95"
❷ EBD=0
  ChangeDir=0
```

**Example 7-3** setup Express Machine Profile

```
❸ OptionalComponents=1
❹ Network=1
   System=0
   CCP=0
   CleanBoot=0
   Display=0
   PenWinWarning=0
   InstallType=3
   DevicePath=0
   ProductID=123456789
❺ TimeZone="Mountain"
   Uninstall=0
   VRC=0
❻ NoPrompt2Boot=1
```

Explanations for several of the entries in the machine profile are provided below[2].

❶    The system files will be copied into the directory c:\win95.

❷    The installation will not prompt for an Emergency Boot Disk (EDB).

❸    Optional components of the distribution will be installed.

❹    The network will be configured.

❺    The Time Zone will be set to "US/Mountain".

❻    The system will re-boot automatically after installation.

### System

In the System area of the machine profile, the display is configured as shown in Example 7-4.

**Example 7-4** Machine Profile – System Area

```
[System]
DisplChar=16,1024,768
```

This example instructs the OS to use a display with 16-bit color depth, and a screen size of 1024 by 768.

### Name and Organization

In Example 7-5, the name of the desktop is set and the organization name is specified in the NameAndOrg area.

**Example 7-5** Machine Profile – NameAndOrg Area

```
[NameAndOrg]
Name="Sales Desktop 1"
Org="My Company Inc."
Display=0
```

2.    See the *Microsoft Office Resource Kit for Windows 95 : The Technical Resource for Installing, Configuring, and Supporting Microsoft Office for Windows 95*, 1995, Microsoft Press. ISBN: 1556158181. This text has full descriptions of machine profile keywords and values.

## Network

The `Network` area of the machine profile is used to configure the network drivers and interfaces, as shown in Example 7-6.

**Example 7-6** Machine Profile – `Network` Area

```
[Network]
ComputerName="columbia-pc"
Workgroup="WORKGROUP"
Description="Vasanthan's Win95 Desktop"
Display=0
PrimaryLogon=VREDIR
Clients=VREDIR, NWREDIR
Protocols=NETBEUI, NWLINK, MSTCP
DefaultProtocol=MSTCP
Services=VSERVER
IgnoreDetectedNetCards=0
ValidateNetCardResources=1
Security=SHARE
```

## Microsoft TCP / IP

Microsoft's implementation of the TCP/IP protocol is configured in the `MSTCP` area of the machine profile, as shown in Example 7-7.

**Example 7-7** Machine Profile – `MSTCP` Area

```
[MSTCP]
LMHOSTPath="C:\WIN95\LMHOSTS"
DHCP=0
DNS=1
WINS=0
DNSServers=129.172.221.1, 129.172.221.239
Domain=Sales.Company.COM
Hostname=columbia-pc
DomainOrder=Sales.Company.COM, Company.COM
IPAddress=129.152.221.224
IPMask=255.255.255.0
```

## Network Drive

In Example 7-8, the first available network drive is assigned to the drive letter F.

**Example 7-8** Machine Profile – NWREDIR Area

```
[NWREDIR]
FirstNetDrive=F:
ProcessLoginScript=1
```

### Software

Non-essential software is selected for installation in the OptionalComponents area of the machine profile, as shown in Example 7-9. The value of 1 indicates that an option is selected, and 0 indicates that it is not selected.

**Example 7-9** Machine Profile – OptionalComponents Area

```
[OptionalComponents]
"Accessibility Options"=1
"Briefcase"=0
"Calculator"=1
"Character Map"=1
"Clipboard Viewer"=1
"Desktop Wallpaper"=1
"Document Templates"=1
"Games"=0
"Mouse Pointers"=1
"Net Watcher"=1
"Object Packager"=1
"Online User's Guide"=1
"Paint"=1
"Quick View"=1
"System Monitor"=1
"System Resource Meter"=1
"Windows 95 Tour"=1
"WordPad"=1
"Dial-Up Networking"=0
"Direct Cable Connection"=0
"HyperTerminal"=1
"Phone Dialer"=1
```

```
"Backup"=0
"Defrag"=1
"Disk compression tools"=1
"Microsoft Exchange"=1
"Microsoft Mail Services"=0
"Microsoft Fax Services"=0
"Microsoft Fax Viewer"=0
"Audio Compression"=1
"CD Player"=1
"Jungle Sound Scheme"=0
"Media Player"=1
"Musica Sound Scheme"=0
"Robotz Sound Scheme"=0
"Sample Sounds"=0
"Sound Recorder"=1
"Utopia Sound Scheme"=0
"Video Compression"=1
"Volume Control"=1
"Additional Screen Savers"=0
"Flying Windows"=1
"The Microsoft Network"=0
```

### *Network Printer*

In Example 7-10, the desktop system's printer queue named `swip` is assigned to a network printer named `myprinter`. This printer is attached to the print server `lanserver` using the LAN Manager/SMB protocol.

**Example 7-10** Machine Profile – `Printers` **area**

```
[Printers]
SWIP=Apple LaserWriter II NTX,\\lanserver\myprinter
```

## Post Installation Configuration

As we mentioned earlier, installing the OS is just one of the activities required before the desktop is ready to operate in the intranet. Usually, there are post-installation tasks, such as creating network mount points and configuring network services, that must also be completed. In this section, we'll describe methods to automate these types of post-installation activities.

### Solaris JumpStart

Besides using profiles to specify disk formatting parameters and the OS software to install, JumpStart can also execute commands before the initial installation begins using a begin script, and after it is completed using a finish script. This capability is useful if you need to preserve files or configuration information, install system or software files, edit system parameters, and perform other configuration tasks.

The post-installation finish script executes after the OS is installed, but before the system is rebooted. The OS packages copied to disk during installation are accessible and can be modified by the post-installation script. To access the file system where the OS is installed, JumpStart uses the special mount point labeled /a. This mount point represents the root (/) directory of the install client. To access the OS and perform modifications, a post-install script simply prefixes /a in the directory path.

Software that is sensitive to the directory path may refuse to install using the /a directory path. For example, the Common Desktop Environment (CDE) installation program searches for the root (/) directory before installing the software. If it is not found, the program exits and the software is not installed. To overcome this limitation, you can use the chroot /a command in the finish script before executing the installation program of a directory path-sensitive software package.

Let's examine some of the typical configuration tasks that can be performed in a post-install script. Example 7-11 shows some common modifications that are performed on a newly-installed system.

**Example 7-11** `post.sh` **JumpStart Post-Installation** `finish` **Script**

```
#!/bin/sh
❶ T=/a

#
# make mail spool directory available locally via NFS
#
❷ rm -rf $T/var/mail
  ln -s /nfs/mailserver/var/spool/mail $T/var/mail

#
# configure desktop to using NIS name service
#
❸ grep -s nisplus $T/etc/nsswitch.conf && {
          cp $T/etc/nsswitch.nis $T/etc/nsswitch.conf
  }

#
# mount /usr/local directory at boot time
#
❹ test -d $T/usr/local || {
  echo "localsrv:/usr/local -  /usr/local nfs 3   yes -" >> $T/etc/vfstab
  mkdir $T/$d
  }
```

The finish script is described below.

❶   Set the value of the variable T to the root (/) directory of the install client.

❷   Enables the client to access the mail spool directory using a symbolic link to an AutoFS-managed NFS mount point.

❸   Configures the install client to use a name service switch file for NIS.

❹   Creates a mount point and modifies the install client vfstab file so the NFS server is mounted at boot time.

Here are some of the more complex configuration activities you can perform using a post-installation script:

•   Create a CacheFS directory

- Mount an NFS server using the CacheFS directory

- Set the root password

- Set up desktop-wide preferences (for example, printing)

- Configure dial-up PPP services

Besides post-installation scripts, JumpStart provides the capability to execute a pre-installation `begin` script before the disks are formatted and partitioned. For example, you can use a pre-install script to preserve files and configuration information to a temporary area before modifying the disk, and you can copy them back to the system after the installation is completed using a post-install `finish` script.

### Windows

Windows also provides post-installation capabilities in two forms. First, you can add directives to the `setup.inf` file to create system registry entries. Secondly, you can add directives to copy files to specific locations.

Example 7-12 provides an instance of the former of these two.

**Example 7-12** Post Installation Using the `setup.inf` File

```
❶ AddReg=MySoft.AddReg
  [MySoft.AddReg]
❷ HKR,Ndi,DeviceID,,NETBEUI
  HKR,Ndi,MaxInstance,,8
```

The `setup.inf` directives are described below.

❶    Define the section `MySoft.AddReg` using the keyword `AddReg`.

❷    Add keys to `HKR` section of the registry in the `MySoft.AddReg` section.

In the following example, the directive `CopyFiles` defines a section `MyFiles.CopyFiles` and then specifies which files to copy into the system folder.

```
CopyFiles=MyFiles.CopyFiles
[MyFiles.CopyFiles]
netbeui.vxd
rpcltc5.dll
rpclts5.dll
```

# Advanced Topics

Let's briefly reiterate the key JumpStart benefits. JumpStart enables you to install and configure desktop computers and server systems in an automated, consistent manner. It helps you avoid common problems associated with distributing OS software, such as OS upgrades and inconsistent system configurations. With JumpStart, you can provide users in your intranet with a more coherent environment to work in. In this section, we'll look at ways to extend JumpStart to provide additional capabilities in your intranet.

### Setting Up a JumpStart Boot Server

If your intranet has multiple subnets, you do not need to set up an install server for each subnet. However, a boot server is required, because the protocol used to boot the install clients (TFTP) does not operate across the subnet boundaries. All that is required for each subnet is a boot server, installed using the `setup_install_server` script.

1.  Log into the boot server as root.

2.  Create the directory to store the boot client files.

```
# mkdir /export/osdist
```

3.  Share the directory.

```
# share -F nfs -o ro /export/osdist
```

**4.**   **Restart the NFS server processes.**

```
# /etc/init.d/nfs.server stop
# /etc/init.d/nfs.server start
```

**5.**   **Set up the boot server.**

```
# /net/install-server/export/osdist/setup_install_server -b /export/osdist
```

In this command, *install-server* is the NFS server that shares the Solaris OS distribution CD (see *Setting Up the Install / Boot Server* on page 80).

You can set up a single machine to provide boot services for multiple subnets. If the server is configured with multiple network interfaces attached to multiple subnets, then that server can provide boot services to the install clients found in all the subnets.

### *Providing Multiple OS Revision Support*

The install server used to provide OS services by sharing the Solaris OS distribution CD can be configured to serve more than one version of the OS. For example, the install server can provide the following revisions of the Solaris software:

- Solaris 2.4

- Solaris 2.5

- Solaris 2.5.1

An install client can be configured to use an existing profile and install any one of the OS revisions listed above. To specify an OS revision for an install client, simply change directory to the appropriate directory and run the add_install_client command, as shown below.

```
# ls -FC /export/osdist
    solaris2.4/ solaris2.5/ solaris2.5.1/
# cd /export/osdist/solaris2.5
# ./add_install_client profile-server:/export/dtprof desktop1 sun4m
```

In this example, *profile-server* is the NFS server that shares the JumpStart profiles (see *Setting Up the Profile Server* on page 81).

In a similar manner, the install server can provide the same revision of the OS for different platforms, such as SPARC and x86.

## Summary

In this chapter, we have looked at ways to avoid a common administration task that is time-consuming, and that can be error-prone and tedious—the task of installing the OS on desktops in the intranet. Fortunately, there are services available (such as Solaris JumpStart) that can automate many of the steps required for OS installation. Though the automated installation method using machine profiles in Windows is not as robust as JumpStart, it can still save time and promotes consistency among desktop OS configurations. In an upcoming chapter, we'll look at how you can avoid the problem of desktop OS installation completely by using zero-administration clients such as AutoClients and JavaStations.

# CHAPTER 8

# Managing Software

## The Software Management Problem

A potentially overwhelming intranet administration task is managing all the software that is installed on desktop computers and server systems. Software management tasks include:

- Software installation
- Software distribution
- Software updates

These tasks must be performed while providing consistent and reliable software services to users. To complicate matters, there are a myriad of other factors to consider when managing software, such as matching software with the right operating system environment and platform and administering software licensing. Given that software is managed in different ways in the Solaris and Windows operating environments, this is an increasingly difficult and time-consuming administration problem. Java-based software eliminates many of these problems, but in this chapter, we'll focus on more traditional types of software and software management methods.

## How Software is Installed

Regardless of the operating system environment, software can be generally be installed on the local hard drive, on the network using a mounted drive, or a combination of both.

### Managing Locally Installed Software

The advantage of installing software locally is that the user has control over the installed software. The disadvantage is that it can place an administrative burden on users that arguably belongs to the administrator. Also, some organizations are fearful of communication breakdowns that result from file and software incompatibilities. Another problem is the liability of individuals using unlicensed, "pirate" copies of software on their desktops. These problems can occur if users manage their own software. For these reasons, the locally-installed model of managing software might suffice for very small organizations, but it quickly becomes difficult to manage as the number of users grows.

### Managing Software on the Network

The next step is to centralize the location of the installed software so that it is shared by multiple users over the network. We'll call this method *managing software on the network*. This software management model is preferable, as it can help to eliminate the software incompatibility and liability problems described earlier. Almost all software on the intranet can be managed over the network, easing software maintenance and update tasks. In this chapter, we'll describe methods of performing network-based software installation and management.

## Solaris Software Management

UNIX environments such as Solaris have traditionally supported a network-based method for software installation. Most UNIX software operates based on the user's search path specified in the `$PATH` environment variable. The user types in a command or accesses a menu command to invoke the software, and the system searches each directory in the search path for the software. When found, the software is invoked. If the software is not found in the search path, the system prints a `command not found` error message.

At a minimum, the following administration tasks are required to enable access to software over the network.

- Mount the software directory

  The NFS distributed file system is used to mount a remote file system so that it appears to be a local file system (for more information, see *Setting Up File Sharing and Printing Services* on page 143).

- Update the search path

  The user's search path is updated to include the mounted software directory, or the network path, as shown below.

---

```
set path = ( /usr/bin /usr/ccs/bin . /network-path )
```

---

The network path enables access to the software. This is a very simple method for managing software, and it is useful mainly for relatively simple, homogenous environments. There are other factors to consider, such as:

- Application-specific user preferences

  This is information that is used to customize the behavior of a software application, such as default printing preferences, color preferences, startup preferences, and so on.

- Software revisions

  Most software applications are continually revised and upgraded. It is possible that files created with one revision of an application are incompatible with another revision.

- Platform/operating system-specific software

  Application software is usually in a binary format intended for a particular processor family, such as Intel *x*86. Application software also has particular operating system environment requirements, such as Solaris 2.5.

- Software licenses

  Licensed software applications employ one of two licensing mechanisms– host-based licensing or server-based licensing. A host-based license is tied to a system, and the software can be used only on that system. A server-based license, also known as a *floating* license, resides on a central server and is shared by multiple systems on a per usage basis.

In a networked Solaris environment, software is installed on servers and made available using NFS mounted directories to the desktop clients. Different revisions of software, supporting different processor platforms and OS versions can be installed on the same network server. The desktops can be configured with the appropriate directories and search paths to access the software.

Most Solaris software is packaged with the following components:

- Default preferences

- Loadable shared libraries

- Executable binaries

- Optional shell scripts optional

The preferred software distribution method is to place all these components in a single directory tree, and then export the directory to intranet desktops using NFS. Collections of software with similar functionality can be grouped into directories, as shown in this example.

```
/usr/openwin (OpenWindows software)
/usr/local (General-purpose software)
/usr/dt (Common Desktop Environment (CDE) software)
/opt/web (Web-based software)
```

Figure 8-1 shows a directory tree structure that is typical for an NFS-exported software directory.

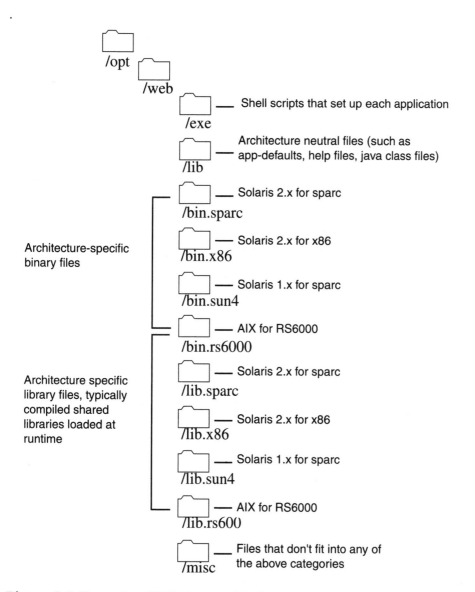

**Figure 8-1** Example – NFS-Exported Software Directory Structure

## Simple Software Management Scenario

To show you how software can be installed and managed over the network, we'll use a scenario. We'll start by showing you how to install the Netscape Navigator software in an intranet that supports a single processor platform and operating system environment. Then, we'll add enhancements such as supporting additional processor platforms and OS environments.

Following is an overview of the initial tasks we'll need to perform:

- Install the software distribution and related files on the server
- Create a shell script called a *wrapper* to manage how the software is invoked by the clients
- Share the software over the network using NFS

### Installing the Software on the Server

The Netscape Navigator 2.0 software for Solaris SPARC is packaged in a compressed `tar` file format and consists of the files described in Table 8-1.

**Table 8-1** Netscape Navigator 2.0 – Solaris 2.x Files

| File | Description |
| --- | --- |
| README | Text file |
| LICENSE | Text file |
| netscape | ELF binary for Solaris 2.x sparc |
| Netscape.ad | X-Window/CDE application defaults |
| XKeysymDB | X-Window/CDE key board mapping |
| libnullplugin.so | SPARC Solaris 2.x shared libraries for plug-ins |
| java_30 | Java class library |

We'll place these files on a single Solaris server, using the directories described in Table 8-2.

**Table 8-2** Netscape Navigator 2.0 File Placement

| Directory Location | File |
| --- | --- |
| /opt/web/lib | README |
| | LICENSE |
| | Netscape.ad |
| | XKeysymDB |

**Table 8-2** Netscape Navigator 2.0 File Placement

| Directory Location | File |
|---|---|
|  | java_30 |
| /opt/web/bin.svr4 | netscape |
| /opt/web/lib.svr4 | libnullplugin.so |

Next, we'll enable client access to the Netscape Navigator software distribution.

### Creating the Software Wrapper

A shell script called a *wrapper* handles the job of starting the Netscape Navigator software properly.

The wrapper handles all the necessary details to ensure the correct version of the software successfully launches on the client system. It does the work of determining the client-specific information (such as the client processor platform and operating environment), and matches this information with the correct binary executable file. The wrapper can be used to perform other administrative tasks, such as setting an environment variable that is required by a software application.

To start, we'll use the wrapper shown in Example 8-1. We'll place the wrapper in the /opt/web/exe directory and name it ns .

**Example 8-1** ns Simple Netscape Navigator Wrapper

```
#!/bin/sh
basedir=/opt/web

PATH=$basedir/exe:$PATH
OPENWINHOME=${OPENWINHOME:-/usr/openwin}
LD_LIBRARY_PATH=$basedir/lib.svr4:$LD_LIBRARY_PATH
XAPPLRESDIR=$basedir/lib
XKEYSYMDB=$basedir/lib/XKeysymDB
CLASSPATH=$basedir/lib/java_30:$CLASSPATH
export PATH OPENWINHOME LD_LIBRARY_PATH XKEYSYMDB XAPPLRESDIR
CLASSPATH

prog=$basedir/bin.svr4/netscape3.0
$prog $*
```

### Sharing the Software

Next, the /opt/web directory needs to be exported with read-only privileges to the desktop clients (see *Setting Up File Sharing and Printing Services* on page 143 for more information). The client systems mount this directory using the /opt/web local mount point.

To run Netscape Navigator, the user then types in this command.

```
% /opt/web/exe/ns
```

These same steps can be performed for multiple desktops, though this process can be automated using Solaris AutoFS (see *Name Services* on page 159 for more information). The benefit of managing software on the network is that many desktop clients can access the software from the same server directory, and you don't have to install the software on each desktop.

### Adding Support for Additional Client Platforms

In this section, we'll extend our software management scenario to include support for multiple processor platforms. Specifically, we'll add support for Intel x86 desktop clients running Solaris 2.*x*.

To add support for this client type, we'll need to perform these tasks:

- Add the Netscape binary for the x86 processor to the bin.x86 directory
- Add the libnullplugin.so file to the lib.x86 directory
- Modify the ns wrapper shell script to support the new platform

In this section, we'll describe each of these tasks.

**1. Create the directory for the new binaries.**

```
# mkdir /opt/web/bin.x86
```

**2. Copy the Netscape binary to the directory.**

```
# cp netscape /opt/web/bin.x86
```

**3.**     **Edit the ns wrapper shell script.**

Add the line arch=`uname -p` and change all occurrences of svr4 to
${arch}. Example 8-2 shows these changes.

**Example 8-2** ns2 **Multi-Platform Netscape Navigator Wrapper**

```
#!/bin/sh
❶ basedir=/opt/web
❷ arch=`uname -p`

PATH=$basedir/exe:$PATH
OPENWINHOME=${OPENWINHOME:-/usr/openwin}
LD_LIBRARY_PATH=$basedir/lib.${arch}:$LD_LIBRARY_PATH
XAPPLRESDIR=$basedir/lib
XKEYSYMDB=$basedir/lib/XKeysymDB
CLASSPATH=$basedir/lib/java_30:$CLASSPATH
export PATH OPENWINHOME LD_LIBRARY_PATH XKEYSYMDB XAPPLRESDIR CLASSPATH
prog=$basedir/bin.${arch}/netscape3.0
❸ $prog $*
```

In ❶, we declare a common directory for the software. The ns wrapper evaluates
the architecture type in ❷, and sets the appropriate environment variables and
finally executes the binary that matches the client processor platform in ❸.

Both the x86 and SPARC-based desktops access the same server directory using
the mount point /opt/web. To start the Netscape Navigator software, each
desktop executes the wrapper by running the /opt/web/exe/ns command.

### Extending the Software Wrapper

Since you control the wrapper, you also control the user environment for starting
the application software. You can change that script in a single, centralized
location on the server, and effectively change the environment and the software
for all users. You also have centralized control for setting environment
preferences and user preferences as well.

For example, you can now set the news server or change the proxy server by simply editing the wrapper, as shown in Example 8-3.

**Example 8-3** ns3 **Enhanced Netscape Navigator Wrapper**

```
#!/bin/sh
basedir=/opt/web
arch=`uname -p`

PATH=$basedir/exe:$PATH
OPENWINHOME=${OPENWINHOME:-/usr/openwin}
LD_LIBRARY_PATH=$basedir/lib.${arch}:$LD_LIBRARY_PATH
XAPPLRESDIR=$basedir/lib
XKEYSYMDB=$basedir/lib/XKeysymDB
CLASSPATH=$basedir/lib/java_30:$CLASSPATH

❶ NNTPSERVER=news.mycompany.com
export PATH OPENWINHOME LD_LIBRARY_PATH XKEYSYMDB XAPPLRESDIR CLASSPATH
NNTPSERVER

pref=$HOME/.netscape/preferences

❷ test -f $pref && {
        ed - $pref <<EOF >/dev/null 2>&1
/^HTTP_PROXY:.*oldproxy/s,oldproxy,newproxy,g
w
q
EOF
}

prog=$basedir/bin.${arch}/netscape
$prog $*
```

In ❶, we set the news server environment variable and export it. In ❷, we add instructions that edit the user's Netscape preferences file and set the proxy server.

### Adding Support for Additional Software Versions

Finally, there often is a need to support multiple versions of a software application from the same software distribution NFS mount point and allow users to choose the version they prefer. This can be implemented using our existing directory structure with some modifications to the wrapper.

Let's assume there is an intranet user who wants to use Netscape Navigator 3.0 for a specific purpose. We can add support for Navigator 3.0 by performing the following tasks.

- Creating version-specific directories under the `lib` directory

  These directories hold version-specific application defaults and README files.

- Naming binaries with file name extensions

  Using a version number for the file name extension enables us to distinguish one version from another.

- Modifying the startup script

  Here, we'll determine the appropriate settings and execute the matching binary.

The new directory structure that includes the Netscape Navigator 3.0 software is described in Table 8-3.

**Table 8-3** Multiple Netscape Version Directory Structure

| Full Pathname | Description |
|---|---|
| /opt/web/lib/2.0/README | 2.0 README file |
| /opt/web/lib/3.0/README | 3.0 README file |
| /opt/web/lib/2.0/Netscape | 2.0 X app-defaults file |
| /opt/web/lib/3.0/Netscape | 3.0 X app-defaults file |
| /opt/web/bin.svr4/netscape3.0 | 3.0 ELF binary for sparc |
| /opt/web/bin.svr4/netscape2.0 | 2.0 ELF binary for sparc |
| /opt/web/bin.x86/netscape3.0 | 3.0 ELF binary for x86 |
| /opt/web/bin.x86/netscape2.0 | 2.0 ELF binary for x86 |
| /opt/web/lib.svr4/libnullplugin.so | 3.0 plugins for sparc |
| /opt/web/lib.x86/libnullplugin.so | 3.0 plugins x86 |
| /opt/web/exe/ns | architecture neutral startup script |

Notice that we created the version-specific directories beneath `/opt/web/lib`, but we did not create another directory for binaries and use a single directory, `/opt/web/bin.svr4`. Instead, we used version-specific file name extensions to distinguish the binaries. Both methods are useful ways to support multiple versions of a software application, and you should use either or both methods wherever appropriate.

Example 8-4 shows the wrapper with the modification to support multiple versions of the Netscape Navigator software.

**Example 8-4** ns4 Revision-Aware Netscape Navigator Wrapper

```
#!/bin/sh
basedir=/opt/web
arch=`uname -p`

PATH=$basedir/exe:$PATH
OPENWINHOME=${OPENWINHOME:-/usr/openwin}
LD_LIBRARY_PATH=$basedir/lib.${arch}:$LD_LIBRARY_PATH
XKEYSYMDB=$basedir/lib/XKeysymDB
NNTPSERVER=news.mycompany.com
export PATH OPENWINHOME LD_LIBRARY_PATH XKEYSYMDB NNTPSERVER

pref=$HOME/.netscape/preferences
test -f $pref && {
        ed - $pref <<EOF >/dev/null 2>&1
/^HTTP_PROXY:.*oldproxy/s,oldproxy,newproxy,g
w
q
EOF
}
getopts "no :$*" o
if [ "$o" = o ]; then
        XAPPLRESDIR=$basedir/lib/netscape/2.0
        CLASSPATH=$basedir/class/moz2_0.zip:$CLASSPATH
        export XAPPLRESDIR CLASSPATH
        prog=$basedir/bin.${arch}/netscape2.0
        shift `expr $OPTIND - 1`
elif [ "$o" = n ]; then
        XAPPLRESDIR=$basedir/lib/netscape/3.0
        CLASSPATH=$basedir/class/java_30:$CLASSPATH
        export XAPPLRESDIR CLASSPATH
        prog=$basedir/bin.${arch}/netscape3.0
        shift `expr $OPTIND - 1`
else
   echo "Usage: $0 [-n(ew 3.0) | -o(ld 2.0)]"
fi
$prog $*
```

## Additional Software Management Requirements

The scenario we just covered described the tasks required to set up and manage software in an NFS-based, Solaris environment. Typically, there are additional requirements for software that is installed and managed in corporate intranets, such as the following:

- Usage monitoring
- Software server replication
- License administration

In this section, we'll look at each of these software management tasks.

### *Usage Monitoring*

Very simple monitoring of software usage can easily be added to the software wrapper. For example, you can add an automatic e-mail message to a predefined usage alias. A more sophisticated technique is submitting an entry to a database each time the software is accessed. Using the versatility of wrappers, either technique can be used to collect a variety of information, such as the following:

- User name
- Desktop configuration
- Start and stop time

### *Server Replication*

Server replication is a good way to balance network loads in busy networks with overloaded NFS servers, improve software access times for a geographically distributed intranet, or simply provide a cushion of redundancy in case of an outage.

In all cases, the `rdist` command can be used to replicate directories such as the entire `/opt/web` directory structure used in our software management scenario to another NFS server across the domain, or to an alternate server used for load balancing purposes.

The following example is an `rdist` script that replicates the `/opt/web` directory structure and `/usr/local` from a central server to the servers `sales` and `mktg`.

**Example 8-5** Simple `rdist` Configuration File

```
HOSTS = (sales mktg)
FILES = (/opt/web /usr/local)
(${FILES}) -> (${HOSTS})
   install -R;
```

The `rdist` command can be scheduled to run at a specific time using the `cron` command. You can also configure `rdist` to send you notifications about failures, updates, and conflicts. It supports a number of other features that add flexibility, such as the following:

- Excluding specific files
- Recursive copying
- Resolving links
- Binary compression

### License Administration

As we described earlier, licensed software applications employ one of two licensing mechanisms– host-based licensing or server-based licensing. A host-based license is tied to a system, and the software can be used only on that system. A server-based license, also known as a *floating* license, resides on a central server and is shared by multiple systems on a per usage basis. By far, this is the preferred method for administering licensed software, as it enables you to control and track software usage in a centralized manner. You can set up secondary license servers to provide software licenses in case the primary license server is unavailable.

In some cases, you can negotiate with the software vendor for a site license. Site-licensed software is easier to administer, since access to the software is guaranteed for all intranet users and a license does not have to be obtained each time the software is invoked.

## Windows Software Management

Unlike Solaris, the Windows environment is oriented towards installing software on the local file system. This presents a problem if we want to centralize software management activities on a network server. In many cases, this limitation can be overcome by installing the software on an NFS mounted network drive (for more information, see *Setting Up File Sharing and Printing Services* on page 143).

Often, installing software in the Windows environment goes beyond copying bits to a drive. Many software applications also install the following types of files to the local drive:

- Shared libraries
- Preferences
- .ini files

These requirements pose a limitation to using software installed on the network on multiple Windows desktops.

Some Windows application software (such as Microsoft Office) supports network installation that separates the networked and local software components, and provides the ability to install only the local components. In this manner, the networked components can be installed on a network drive and shared with other PC desktops since the entire software distribution can be placed on a network drive. PC desktop users can browse and run the setup program using local-only installation mode, and they can direct the software setup program to use the network components.

Software management tools (such as Solstice PC-Software Director[1] and Solstice PC-Admin[2]) give you the ability to install software using the setup program from a remote desktop, thus enabling you to install local software components on users' desktops from a centralized location, your administration machine.

### The Windows Registry

The newest PC-based operating systems store all user and application settings in a single, local database called the *registry*. The Windows registry stores the settings that are specific to the desktop, or to the user. There is a user-specific area and a system specific area for settings. However, dynamically loadable libraries (DLLs) must still be installed locally.

Windows NT also provides you with the ability to edit registries residing on individual PC desktops from a remote machine. This capability is optional in Windows 95 and must be enabled by the administrator.

---

1. For more information, visit http://www.sun.com/sunsoft/solstice/Networking-products/pcswdir.html/.
2. For more information, visit http://www.sun.com/sunsoft/solstice/Networking-products/PC-Admin.html/.

## Summary

There are advantages and disadvantages to managing software on the network using the centralized software distribution model. Obviously, the access time on a network disk is slower than the time spent accessing a local disk, though this can be barely perceptible to a user in an uncongested local area network, or even a high-speed wide area network. However, the ability to store and update the software from a single location is powerful, convenient, and outweighs the disadvantage of slightly slower access times. Caching technologies such as Solaris CacheFS and PC-CacheFS[3] have improved access times to the point that speed is no longer an issue in a centralized software distribution environment.

The greatest advantage to managing software over the network is the cost savings over managing software locally. This is especially evident in a corporate intranet, where the savings are magnified by the thousands of desktops with software access needs.

3.    For more information, visit http://www.sun.com/sunsoft/solstice/em-products/system/pccache/PCCacheFS.html/. A demo is available.

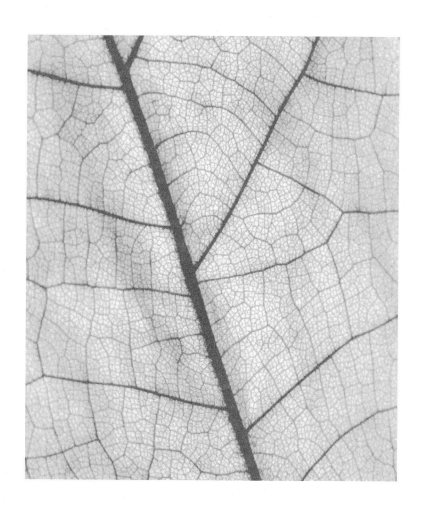

# CHAPTER 9

# Setting Up User Accounts

O ne of the important intranet administration tasks is creating and managing user accounts. In Solaris and Windows, access to computing resources is controlled through user accounts. Critical intranet services such as file sharing and e-mail rely on user account information such as the user ID (UID) to allow or deny access to files, and to send and receive e-mail, respectively. A user account is usually linked to a home directory, where users store data, application preferences, and other information, such as home pages. In this chapter, we'll describe the elements that comprise a user account, and we'll present guidelines for efficient user account administration.

## What is a User Account?

User accounts in Solaris and Windows NT use the following account-related mechanisms:

- Login name

  The login name is an easily-remembered string, such as lou or vasa.

- Password

  The password is an encrypted string of at least six case-sensitive, alpha-numeric characters.

- Group

  A group is used to control access to files and directories. For example, a user might have to be a member of the `staff` group in order to view the contents of a directory that allows read access only to members of this group.

- Account expiration date

  To avoid security problems such as unauthorized access, an account expiration date can be used to deactivate a user account after a specified period.

- Default directory

  Also known as home directory, the default directory is used to store user-specific files such as application preferences, user data, and so on.

In Solaris, user accounts are also associated with a login shell, also known as the default shell. User accounts are represented in the operating environment by a number known as user ID or UID, and they are often associated with a group, which is also represented by a group ID or GID. The UID and GID are used for file and directory access privileges.

User accounts in Solaris and Windows NT share almost all the characteristics we've just mentioned, but Windows 95 user accounts have only minimal features. Unless otherwise noted, the user account topics described in the chapter apply to both Solaris and Windows NT. We'll explicitly call out the Windows 95 differences.

## Solaris User Accounts

In Solaris, the home directory is used to store user-specific preferences besides the user name, group, and password. The path name to the home directory is denoted using `~/`. Here are several of the files stored in the home directory that are used to store the user's application-specific preferences:

- `~/.cshrc`
- `~/.login`

  These files contain a set of commands to be executed upon login to set the working environment and indicate search paths, default printers, and so on.

- `~/.Xdefaults`

  This file contains preferences used by the X-Windows window environment.

- `~/.dt`

  This directory contains preferences for the Common Desktop Environment (CDE).

In an intranet setting, where file sharing and naming services enable the user to access the home directory from any desktop, these files contain the preferences that are available to the user throughout the intranet. The user has the same access to resources such as mail, printing, and file sharing regardless of the particular system the user is logged into. As long as that system shares the name space information to which the user belongs, the user has universal access to intranet resources (see *Name Services* on page 159).

In Solaris, there are preference files that are stored on the local system that can augment or override the preferences stored in the user's home directory. These files include:

- `/etc/.login`

  This file sets the defaults for C-shell users.

- `$OPENWINHOME/server/etc/OWconfig`

  This file sets the defaults for the OpenWindows window environment.

- `/usr/openwin/lib/Xdefaults`

  This file sets the defaults for the X-Windows window environment.

## Centralized Solaris User Account Management

Using the NIS directory service, the NFS file sharing service, and AutoFS, you can greatly simplify user account administration while providing enhanced levels of service to users. Let's recap the benefits of each of these services:

- NIS

  A directory service that enables the centralized administration of configuration information with distributed access.

- NFS

  A file sharing service that enables desktops to access remote file systems as if they were local.

- AutoFS

  Complimentary NFS service that automatically mounts the NFS resources on demand, and unmounts these resources after a specified period of inactivity.

Following is an overview of how intranet services work together to provide user login and home directory services:

1.  The user types in the login and password.

**2.** The user is authenticated using the NIS `passwd` database.
Users can login to the network from any host. The NIS service stores user login and password information, and authenticates the user.

**3.** The user's home directory location is obtained from the NIS `auto_home` map using `AutoFS`. The path to the user's home directory is specified as /home/*login-name*.

**4.** The user's home directory is automatically mounted from the centralized home directory server using `NFS`.

**5.** The user accesses the home directory and completes the login process.

The key concept in this scenario is that critical components such as the user's login and home directory information are managed in a centralized manner using a server-centric computing model. Because this information is not tied to a single desktop, it enables the availability of home directories on all the desktops in the intranet under a uniform name space regardless of their physical locations.

Another important advantage is that the centralized physical location of home directories enables easy backup, recovery, and other administration tasks.

## Solaris User Account Management Recommendations

In this section, we'll present guidelines for efficient user account administration.

### Centralize Account Creation

You can set up new user accounts from anywhere in the intranet using the NIS or NIS+ name service. The following user parameters can be centrally administered and maintained. The user's preferences will be maintained regardless of the host the user chooses to login to, as long as the host is a member of the name space.

- Password
- Password expiration date
- Home directory location
- Mail file location
- Calendar file location
- User name
- E-mail address
- Default shell
- Default environment

If the user is transferred to a different physical location within the intranet, the preferences travel with that user.

### Plan for Growth

If you anticipate users moving between name service domains, make sure that account creation is unique across domains to avoid name space conflicts.

### Use a Common User Identification Scheme

For example, use the employee's badge number as the User ID. Ensure the user has a unique login name, so the user can move across domains without any conflicts.

A user's login doesn't have to be the user's e-mail address. Use a name service like NIS to map the user's login to an address that has an easy-to-use format, such as `first.last@domain`. You can use the Database Manager to modify the NIS aliases database and map a user login to an e-mail address (see *Setting Up E-mail Services* on page 201).

### Create User Profiles

User profiles help save time by avoiding unnecessary customization of individual user environments, and they promote consistency across a workgroup. Create a custom user profile for a particular type of user, and use this profile when adding a new user. You can specify preferences such as the default printer and shell search path in a user preference file such as the `.cshrc` or `.login` file (see *Solaris User Accounts* on page 118). Create a separate directory for each profile on a centrally-accessible server, and populate the directory with the preferences files suited for that user profile. When you add a new user, you can specify the network path to the user profile directory, and the preferences will be copied to the user's home directory. The user profile directory is also known as the *skeleton* directory.

### Establish a Name Service Policy

A Solaris user account can be enabled on a desktop using the locally stored `/etc/passwd` database, or it can be enabled in a centralized manner using the NIS or NIS+ name service. NIS and NIS+ are name services that operate like a global name service database. They enable users to access their environment from any intranet desktop. Here are some of the advantages to maintaining user accounts using a name service:

- Centralized management

    All user accounts can be controlled and managed from a single desktop.

- File sharing

    Network file sharing can be administered without any conflicts.

- Ease of use

  Roaming users can access their home directories from any desktop in the intranet.

There are added advantages such as global e-mail accounts, mail delivery to fixed location, and so on.

When an intranet site has more than one desktop, it becomes essential to use a global name service such as NIS. The NIS or NIS+ name service can be enabled on any Solaris desktop using the `/etc/nsswitch.conf` file. This file determines the order in which name services such as NIS and DNS are used to resolve lookups for the user account, host information, and so on. Normally, this file is configured when the Solaris system is installed. Afterwards, you can easily change the lookup policy using the template files described in Table 9-1.

**Table 9-1** Name Service Switch Configuration File Templates

| Configuration File | Description |
|---|---|
| `/etc/nsswitch.files` | Use local files only |
| `/etc/nsswitch.nis` | Use the NIS name service |
| `/etc/nsswitch.nisplus` | Use the NIS+ name service |

To change the lookup policy, copy the appropriate template to `/etc/nsswitch.conf` and reboot the system (we'll assume you already have set up NIS services. For more information on how to set up NIS services, consult the documentation that came with your system).

### Use a Home Directory Server

In the Solaris environment, user-specific files are stored in the user's default directory, the home directory. Usually, it's preferable to store home directories in a centralized manner on a home directory server and use NFS to access the home directory from each desktop. The names and locations of home directories are stored in NIS in a uniform manner to allow seamless access for all users.

Designate an NFS server with adequate diskspace in the `/export/home` directory as the home directory server. A general rule of thumb is to allocate 200 Mbytes of disk space for each user, though the actual disk space requirements vary depending on the environment.

## Solaris User Account Administration Tools

You can use the command line interface to create a new user account in Solaris by manually editing configuration files such as /etc/passwd and /etc/shadow. This practice is discouraged, as it provides no error or consistency checking. Other commands (such as user_add and group_add) can be used to safely add a new user account, but they are useful only when adding a user to the local system, and they are not integrated with NIS or NIS+.

Because of these limitations, the recommended method to create a user account is to use Solstice AdminSuite. AdminSuite offers an easy-to-use GUI for performing common administration tasks such as creating, deleting, and modifying user accounts, is fully integrated with NIS and NIS+, and provides error checking capabilities. An added benefit is that you can use AdminSuite from any desktop in the intranet.

AdminSuite is bundled with Solaris server kits. If you have not purchased this software, you can use the bundled Administration Tool, /bin/admintool. Administration Tool is like a light version of AdminSuite — you can't administer either the NIS or NIS+ name service, however.

## Additional Solaris User Account Creation Activities

There are several other associated tasks involved in creating a user account, specifically:

- Managing e-mail accounts
- Managing disk quotas
- Managing access permissions

These are largely site policy issues, and vary depending on your needs. In this section, we'll describe each of these topics.

### E-mail Accounts

By default, an e-mail account uses the following format.

```
login-name@desktop.company.com
```

E-mail can be configured to be delivered to a user's desktop's mail spool file. However, for easier administration, e-mail accounts that are represented as mail spool files should be centralized and e-mail addresses should use a canonical form, an often-used format that scales well with growth. An example is shown below.

```
FirstName.Middleinitial.LastName@<Site>.Company.COM
```

Using this e-mail address format, you can reduce the chances of name space conflicts, and users don't have to remember the obscure login name abbreviations, plus the mail spool files can be backed up in a centralized location. All this can be done using a site wide alias file. For details on how to set up e-mail aliases, see *Setting Up E-mail Services* on page 201.

### Disk Quotas

The preferred method of managing home directories is to centralize them on an NFS server. When a file system is shared by many users, all the available disk space can be used at times, and work is temporarily halted until disk space becomes available. Users sometimes fill up their home directories with old and unused files, further exacerbating the problem.

Most administrators solve this problem by placing users on disks based on their work patterns and growth needs, and avoid the use of disk quotas. A disk quota limits the disk space available for users. If there is a need to limit the use of available disk space due to limited resources, cost, and so on, quotas can be deployed. For example, an internet service provider may want to allocate disk space based on the service class of the customer, or a university may want to enforce disk quotas for transient student accounts.

### Solaris Access Permissions

Most Solaris users are familiar with the file permission and ownership flags described in Table 9-2.

**Table 9-2** Permission / Ownership Flags

| Permission/Ownership Flag | Meaning |
|---|---|
| r | Readable |
| w | Writable |
| x | Executable |

**Table 9-2** Permission / Ownership Flags  (Continued)

| Permission/Ownership Flag | Meaning |
| --- | --- |
| u | User |
| g | Group |
| o | Others |

Permissions are changed using the chmod(1) command, and ownership is changed with the chown(1) command. The default permissions on newly created files and directories are controlled using the umask(1) command in the user's startup shell environment. You can override this setting in the /etc/cshrc or /etc/login file to protect naive users from exposing their files. Similarly, users can override these setting in their shell preferences file. The following example should help explain this concept:

```
% umask 022
% mkdir dir1;ls -ld dir1
drwxr-xr-x   2 user      staff            69 Oct 27 22:04 dir1
% touch file1;ls -l file1
-rw-r--r--   1 user      staff             0 Oct 27 22:04 file1
% umask 002
% mkdir dir2;ls -ld dir2
drwxrwxr-x   2 user      staff            69 Oct 27 22:05 dir2
% touch file2;ls -l file2
-rw-rw-r--   1 user      staff             0 Oct 27 22:05 file2
```

Using an umask value of 022, all new files are readable to the owner, group, and others, and all directories are listable to them as well. With the umask set to 002, the owner and group have read and write access to file and directories.

## Creating Solaris User Accounts

*Prerequisites*

This section describes how to create new user accounts in a Solaris environment that has NIS or NIS+ name services available. If you need more information about how to set up NIS or NIS+, consult the documentation that came with your system.

*Overview*

This is an overview of the tasks involved in creating user accounts in Solaris.

- Set up the home directory server
- Create the user account using User Manager
- Configure the AutoFS map in the name service (optional)
- Set up disk quotas (optional)

This procedure describes how to add a user account using AdminSuite.

### Setting Up the Home Directory Server

1.  Log into the designated home directory server as root.

2.  Export the `/export/home` directory for read and write access.

```
# share -o rw access=hostA:hostB /export/home
```

You should also edit the `/etc/dfs/dfstab` file and add this entry to ensure the directory remains exported after a system reboot.

Notice that access is limited to the specified hosts *hostA*, *hostB*, and so on. This is to limit access to the home directories stored on the server. To simplify host access control, you can use a netgroup, or a collection of hosts.

### Creating the User Account

1.  **Make sure you are logged in as a user belonging to the sysadmin user group.**
    To verify that you are a member of the `sysadmin` group, type `groups` and see if you belong to the `admin` group. AdminSuite requires membership in this group in order to perform system administration tasks on remote systems.

2.  **Start the Solstice Launcher.**

```
% /bin/solstice
```

The Solstice Launcher window is displayed.

3. **Click on the User Manager button.**

The Load naming service window is displayed. An example is shown below.

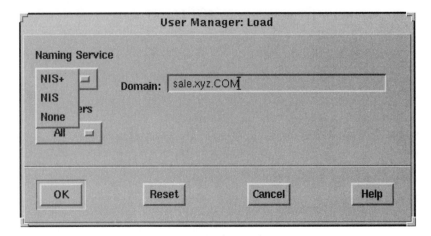

4. **Select a naming service and click OK.**

The User Manager window is displayed. An example is shown below.

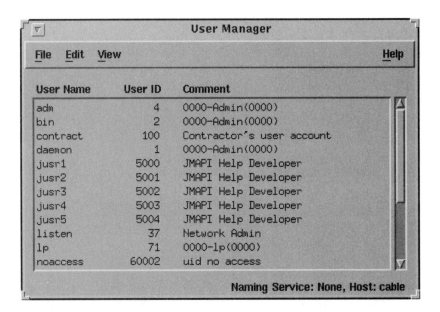

**5.** Select Edit ➤ Add menu to fill in the user identity.
The Add user window is displayed.

To provide you with some assistance in completing the add user form, we've included a brief description of important user properties in Table 9-3.

**Table 9-3** Solaris User Properties

| User Property | Description |
|---|---|
| User Name | A user name (8 characters or less). This can be a unique abbreviation of the user's real name. |
| User ID | A UID can be an ordered, unique number, such as the user's employee number. |
| Password | The password can be left for the user to assign (they are prompted for a new password when they first log in). |
| Groups | You can associate the user with any existing groups (such as sales, staff, admin, and so on) and grant the user privileges associated with those groups. New groups can be created using Group Manager. |
| Login Shell | The user's startup environment. Usually, this is the C-shell (/bin/csh), Bourne shell (/bin/sh), or Korn shell (/bin/ksh). |
| Home Directory | This path to the user's home directory normally uses the /home/*user-name* path name. |
| Home Directory Server | This is the system where the home directory is stored. Ideally, this a centralized NFS server. |
| Skeleton Path | This is the path to the profile directory containing customized user-preference files such as .cshrc and .profile. |
| Auto Home Setup | This option enables home directory access from any desktop using the NIS auto_home map. |
| Mail Server | The mail server specified in this field is used to create an entry in the mail aliases database. |

Other fields such as password expiration can be implemented according to your site policy.

If you checked the auto_home setup option and specified the home directory server, the account is ready for use. User Manager automatically performs the updates to NIS to enable the user account. If you did not specify the `auto_home` setup option, there are additional tasks remaining before the user can access the account. Specifically, the NIS maps must be configured.

**6.   Fill out the form, and click OK.**

The Add user window is dismissed, and the User Manager window reflects a pending transaction.

**7.   Select File ➤ Save Changes in the User Manager window.**

The user is added.

### *Configuring The NIS* `auto_home` *Map*

This procedure is required only if you did not use the `auto_home` setup feature in User Manager when creating the user account.

**1.   Log into the NIS server as root.**

**2.   Add the following lines to the** `/etc/auto_master` **file.**

```
/home auto_home -intr
```

You can specify any NFS options that you need in this file, such as `noquota,nosuid,soft,timeo`.

**3.   Add entries to the** `/etc/auto_home` **file for each user.**

```
user1    hdserver1:/export/home/&
user2    hdserver2:/bigdisk/home/&
```

The first entry designates `user1`'s home directory server as `hdserver1` and its location as `/export/home/user1`. The `&` character is a keyword that is substituted with the user's login name by the NIS server. Similarly, the second entry designates `user2`'s home directory as located at `/bigdisk/home/user2` on `hdserver2`.

**4.   Rebuild the NIS maps.**

```
# cd /var/yp;make
```

**5.**   **Verify that the auto_home map is updated.**

An example is shown below.

```
# ypmatch -k user1 auto_home
user1  hdserver1:/export/home/user1
```

Each user name has a corresponding entry in the `auto_home` map. The `auto_home` map also allows you to specify multiple home directory servers. The advantage to storing home directory information in NIS is a consistent name space. When the user logs in, the system verifies the user entry in the NIS maps, checks for the password, locates the home directory using the `auto_home` map, and mounts the home directory using AutoFS.

### Setting Up Disk Quotas for Solaris Users

A disk quota is enabled on the machine where the UNIX File System (UFS) physically resides. This is usually the home directory server, but it can also be the mail server where the user's mail spool file is stored, typically the `/var/mail` directory.

This procedure describes how to enable optional disk quotas on a UFS file system.

**1.**   **Log into the host where you want to establish the disk quota as root.**

**2.**   **Create the quota for the file system.**

```
# touch UFS-mountpoint/quota
```

On a home directory server, the UFS mount point is usually `/export/home`.

**3.**   **Establish a disk quota for each user.**

```
# edquota -t
```

Add the disk size and grace period for each user.

**4.    Turn on the disk quotas.**

```
# quotaon
```

Quotas are also enabled when the system is rebooted.

You can verify current quotas using the `quotacheck` command and generate a report of usage using the `repquota` command. To view used and available disk space, use the `df -k` command.

# Windows User Accounts

Windows user-specific preferences are stored in the system registry. Two hierarchies in the system registry named `HKEY_CURRENT_USER` and `HKEY_USERS` store user preference information.

Unlike the NIS or NIS+ name services found in Solaris, the registry is specific to the desktop PC, and it is stored on the local disk. However, the registry can be accessed from a remote machine, enabling the administrator to modify portions of the registry and make changes to the user name space.

This registry file can be accessed on different machines in the network, enabling access to resources such as mail, printing, and file sharing regardless of the particular system the user is currently logged onto.

A capability for setting user preferences similar to the `.cshrc` and `.login` files in Solaris and other UNIX-based operating environments also exists in Windows NT. Windows NT permits the execution of user-specific scripts using the `profile` directory.

Global, system-wide preferences such as those stored in the `/etc/.login` file in Solaris can also be enabled in Windows.

All of these methods are ways to define the name space of the working environment for users.

## Windows User Account Administration Tools

- Windows 95

   The Windows 95 operating environment offers administration tools to manage user accounts, but these operate on a per-machine basis.

- Windows NT

   The Windows NT operating environment allows you to create user accounts on the server and enable network logins.

### *Windows User Authentication*

* Windows NT

   In a network login, the user logs into any host in the Windows NT domain and is authenticated by the NT server system, and the user is allowed to log into the NT workstation.

### *Solaris and Windows NT Interoperability*

User login and authentication services can't be shared between Windows NT and Solaris. Windows NT cannot use NIS name services to authenticate users, and the Solaris environment cannot access NT authentication services either.

## Windows NT User Accounts

Most of the Solaris user account concepts we discussed apply to Windows NT also. The Windows NT User Manager allows users with Administrator privileges to create user accounts. User accounts can be created on the local desktop, or they can be created on a Windows NT domain server.

User name choices can be similar to user names in the Solaris environment. Password assignment can be left to the user upon first login, or you can use stricter parameters for password selection, such as using a combination of case-sensitive and alpha-numeric characters.

By default, user home directories are maintained in the following directory location.

```
system_directory\Profiles\user-name
```

An example is shown below.

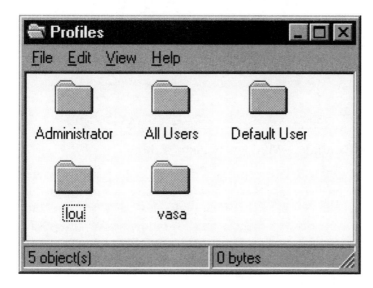

Similar to Solaris, these directories can be centrally maintained on a server and can accessed from desktops using a file sharing service such as PC-NFS or LAN Manager.

The concept of a Solaris UID appears in Windows NT in the form of the SID. Unlike the Solaris environment, the SID is automatically assigned when the user is created. You don't have much choice in choosing a SID. This information is kept in the registry under the following field.

```
HKEY_LOCAL_MACHINE\SOFTWARE\Microsoft\WindowsNT\CurrentVersion\ProfileList
```

You can use the Windows `regedit` utility to browse the registry. An example is shown in Figure 9-1.

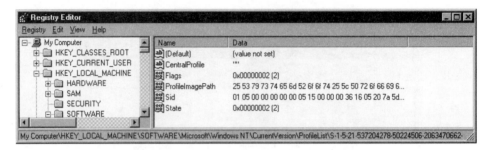

**Figure 9-1** Example – Windows Registry Editor

Another similarity to Solaris appears in the manner that user preferences are stored in Windows NT. Like Solaris, user preferences are maintained in the home directories, enabling users to carry their preferences such software settings, menu items and login scripts with them as they log onto other Windows NT desktops. Also like Solaris, users can't log in to a Windows NT desktop without an account.

## Windows 95 User Accounts

The Windows 95 environment has a loosely defined concept of user—you don't need a user account to log in to a Windows 95 desktop, for example. By simply canceling the login window, you can log in to a Windows 95 desktop. However, a login is necessary when using a network resource such as a file sharing service. By default, user home directories are not enabled on a Windows 95 desktop.

Windows 95 login authentication can be accomplished using a Windows NT domain server or a Netware server.

Typically, Windows 95 user account information is stored in the local machine's registry. There is no concept of UIDs in Windows 95, and the user name is reflected in file ownership and password information is stored in *username*.pwl files in the System_dir (C:\Windows) directory.

## Creating Windows NT User Accounts

1.  **Log into the Windows NT server or Windows NT Workstation as Administrator.**

2.  **Select Start ➤ Programs ➤ Administration Tools (Common) ➤ User Manager for Domains.**
    The User Manager window appears, as shown in the following example.

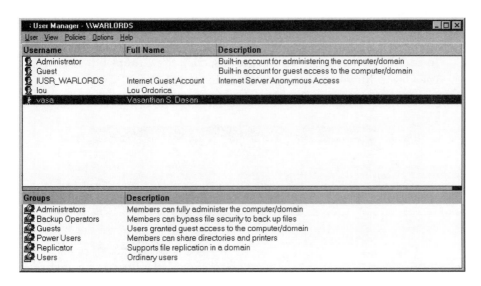

3. **Select User ➤ New User.**

   The New User window is displayed.

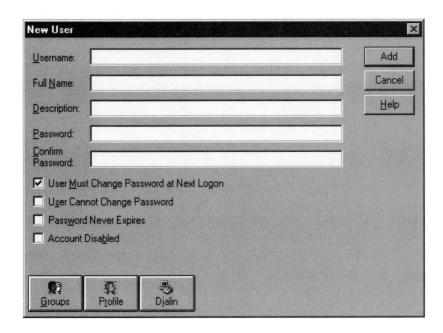

4. **Fill out the form.**
   Click Help if you require additional information to complete the new user fields.

5. **To add the new user to existing groups, click the Groups button.**
   The Group Memberships window is displayed.

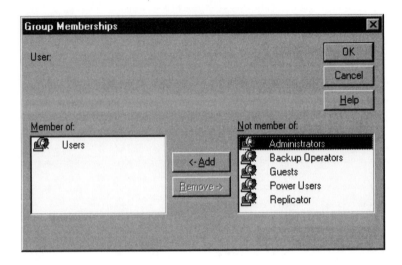

6. **Add the group memberships, and click OK.**

7. **To use an existing profile for the new user, click the Profile button.**
   The User Environment Profile window is displayed.

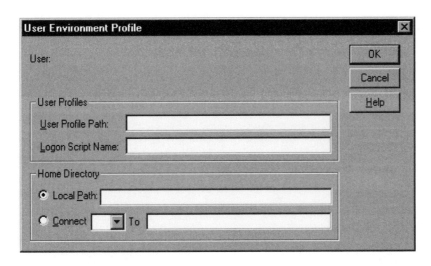

8.  **Fill out the form, and click OK.**
    Click Help if you require additional information to complete the fields.

9.  **Click Add.**
    The new user is added.

## Enabling the Windows 95 User Password

1.  **Select Start ➤ Settings ➤ Control Panel ➤ Password.**
    The Passwords Properties window is displayed.

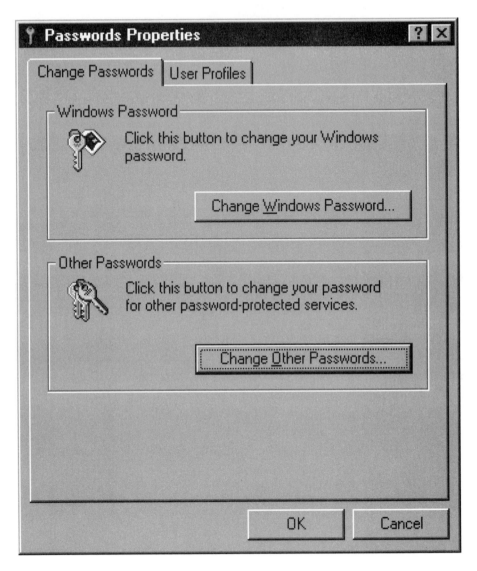

2.   Click Change Windows Password.

3.   Enter the password and user information.

## Summary

The Windows environment is intended for a single user desktop setting. Unlike Solaris, home directories are rarely found in the PC environment. User files are usually stored on the local hard disk, creating a management problem since backing up and recovering these files can be a difficult and time-consuming task. These problems are not limited to Windows—they can also arise in a Solaris environment. To avoid these problems, take care to ensure that user accounts are set up in a server-centric manner using the techniques described in this chapter.

# CHAPTER
# 10

# Setting Up File Sharing and Printing Services

**F**ile sharing is the ubiquitous client/server application that enables users to access files stored in a centralized, manageable location using a unified name space. With file sharing, a client such as a desktop computer accesses a remote file system on a server as if it were a local file system. File sharing offers the following data management advantages to the intranet:

- Data is easily distributed to client systems.

- Data is easier to manage since it is stored in a centralized manner. For example, centralized data is easier to back up.

- Users have a consistent view of the data, since files can be accessed using an easy-to-use, simplified name space.

In this chapter, we'll describe how to implement heterogenous file sharing services based on the NFS distributed file system, the de-facto standard file sharing protocol.

## What is NFS?

Developed in 1986, NFS allows file systems physically located on different machines to be shared by other machines over the network. NFS[1] is available for almost all major operating system environments, including Windows. NFS server and client capabilities are provided in Solaris, and other UNIX-based operating system environments, such as HP-UX, AIX, and SCO.

### NFS File Sharing Uses

With NFS, clients can perform both read and write operations on files. For now, let's focus on the capabilities offered by read-only access. Here are a few examples of how read-only file access is used in an intranet:

- Clients access and run software applications that are too large to reside on the local disk.

- Clients access software applications without having to configure the applications, since they are installed and configured centrally on the file server. The user may have a set of application preferences stored in the workspace for applications that are accessed using a file sharing service.

- Clients access centralized information that changes frequently, such as design specifications, project plans, programming libraries, and so on.

- An administrator installs, updates, and configures software once on a server, and the software is immediately made available to all the clients.

### Scaling NFS

A single NFS server can support multiple clients on the network. The total number of clients supported by an NFS server depends on the type and number of NFS activities. NFS network traffic includes the following operations:

- Writes
- Reads
- Lookups
- Attribute checking
- Retransmissions

1. For more information, visit
   http://www.cis.ohio-state.edu/htbin/rfc/rfc1094.html/.

The following factors affect NFS throughput and performance:

- Number of clients connected to the NFS server
- Network activity
- Client memory and disk configuration

You can increase the number of clients supported by an NFS[2] server by tuning the server, client, or network. In a similar fashion, you can also increase the NFS performance for the clients, or you can balance network loads.

For example, by implementing file caching on NFS clients, you can reduce server and network load and increase the number of clients the server supports. File caching keeps a copy of data accessed over the network in local storage so that it can be quickly and easily accessed. Instead of accessing the server, clients access the cache, conserving server and network resources. Better server performance is a side-effect of using caching.

CacheFS is a technology available in Solaris that enables the caching on an NFS client. This capability is also available in the PC-CacheFS[3] product for Windows for Workgroups 3.*x* and Windows 95.

## Heterogenous File Sharing Services

Several software companies[4] offer products that enable the Windows client with NFS client capabilities. Even without NFS client software, a Windows desktop can use LAN Manager, the native file sharing service provided in Windows, to access a Solaris server. This is accomplished by configuring the server with specialized software that enables the Solaris server to interoperate with the LAN Manager protocol. To the Windows desktop, the Solaris server appears to be a regular LAN Manager file server, and users can easily access the server using the Microsoft Network Neighborhood.

2.  For more information on tuning NFS servers, see *Managing NFS and NIS,* by Hal Stern. O'Reilly and Associates, Inc. ISBN:0-937175-75-7.
3.  For more information, see the URL http://www.sun.com/sunsoft/solstice/em-products/system/pccache/PCCacheFS.html/.
4.  For a list of companies that provide NFS software for Windows, visit http://www.sun.com/sunsoft/solaris/desktop/nfs.html/.

There are commercial and public-domain solutions that enable this type of heterogenous file sharing service in an intranet:

- Solstice Network Client

  This commercial product enables a Solaris server to use the NIS name service to serve files to Windows 95 clients. With Solstice Network Client, a Windows user can seamlessly access files from a Solaris server using the Microsoft Network Neighborhood. File ownership information is managed using the NIS name service. This product also uses caching to improve performance for Windows users and reduce network and server loads.

- Samba

  This public domain software enables a Solaris server to provide file sharing services to Windows clients using the Windows LAN Manager protocol . Though files are stored on the Solaris server using the UNIX file system (UFS) type, they appear to clients as native Windows files. Samba uses the NIS name service for information such as the user login and password to grant file sharing access to Windows users.

### Heterogenous File Sharing Limitations

There are several potential problem areas that you need to be aware of when you use a heterogenous file sharing service such as Samba.

- User Identification (UID)

  The UID and user login identity is used to map ownership information for the files stored in the file system. An interoperability problem arises in that UID and user information is not shared between the Windows and Solaris environments. A user on an NT workstation that accesses a file owned by a user in the Solaris name space cannot properly map the owner's UID to the user login, and vice-versa. For this reason, the Windows user account information must match the information stored in NIS.

- File names

  An interoperability problem arises in that file name lengths are not consistent between the Solaris and Windows. The Solaris supports file names up to 256 characters long, as does the Windows NT operating environment. However, the Windows 95 operating environment maps long file names internally to MS-DOS-style, 8.3 character format. This mapping is stored internally in the Windows 95 operating environment, and it is not accessible from Solaris.

- Reserved file name characters

  Certain characters used in file names in the Solaris are not permissible in Windows.

## The Samba File Sharing and Printing Service

Samba[5] is a suite of programs that enables Windows clients to access resources that reside on a machine that doesn't run Windows, such as a Solaris server. As we discussed earlier, Windows systems use a native file access protocol called LAN Manager, also known as Session Message Block (SMB). This means the intranet desktops running Windows for Workgroups, Windows 95, Windows NT, or OS/2 can access UNIX File System (UFS) files using the native SMB file protocol.

The administrative advantage is that Windows desktops don't need any additional networking software to access resources on a non-Windows server. They use bundled networking software to access both Windows resources and non-Windows resources. Additionally, data can be maintained on a reliable, centralized location—the Solaris server. Data is backed up conveniently, while providing access to Windows desktops.

Besides providing Windows clients with access to Solaris UFS resources, Samba also provides access to print queues on those Solaris servers as well. This enables Windows users to configure a printer using native tools such as the Add Printer Wizard so they can print local and remote files. The Windows print jobs are queued to the Solaris server, and they are printed like regular Solaris print jobs.

## Setting Up Heterogenous File Sharing Services

To describe how to set up read-only NFS file sharing services, we'll use a scenario. XYZ Graphics is a workgroup sized intranet that has a file sharing need. The company must provide access to artwork that is commonly used in projects to all users running both Windows and Solaris, as shown in Figure 10-1.

---

5. For more information, visit http://samba.canberra.edu.au/ and news:comp.protocols.smb.

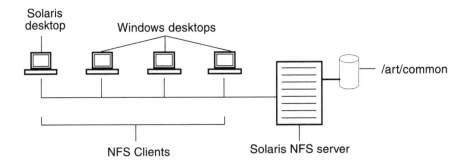

**Figure 10-1** Example – NFS Client/Server Configuration

In this scenario, the directory /art/common is located in a local file system on the Solaris server. To share this directory and its contents with the client systems, we'll configure heterogenous NFS file sharing services on the Solaris server.

This is an overview of the procedure for setting up heterogenous file sharing services.

- Mount the local disk and create the directory on the Solaris server
- Set up NFS services and export the directory on the Solaris server
- Set up the Solaris NFS client
- Set up Samba services on the Solaris server
- Set up the Windows LAN Manager client

### Configuring the NFS Server

1. **Log into the server as root.**
2. **Mount the local, disk-based file system.**
3. **Start NFS services.**

```
# /etc/init.d/nfs.server start
```

4. **Edit the file sharing configuration table so that the directory is shared even after the system is rebooted.**
   Add the following lines to the /etc/dfs/dfstab file.

```
share -F nfs -o ro /art/common
```

**5.**   **Next, export the file system.**

```
# shareall
```

Complete this step, and you're done.

### Configuring the Solaris NFS Client

The Solaris client requires no configuration to access the NFS resource—the exported directory is immediately available using AutoFS. To access the exported directory, the client simply changes the directory using the special /net path name, as shown below:

```
% cd /net/file-server/common/art
```

Optionally, the client file system table /etc/vfstab can be edited so the NFS resource is always mounted even after the system is rebooted:.

```
file-server:/art/common - /local-mnt-point nfs - yes -
```

A preferred method is to use a naming service such as NIS to store NFS resource information. Using a naming service improves the ease of access for users, and it also enables easier administration, since the administrative data is maintained centrally and automatically distributed to clients over the network. For more information, see *Name Services* on page 159.

### Configuring the Samba Server

This is an overview of the procedure for setting up Samba services.

* Obtain the Samba software

* Install and configure the Samba software

Each of these tasks is performed on the Solaris server. Once the Samba software is installed and configured on the server, it looks just like a regular Windows server to the Windows clients on the network.

**Obtaining the Samba Software**

**1.**   **Log into the designated server as root.**

2.  **Obtain the latest Samba software distribution.**
    You can download a copy of the software from the Internet using
    anonymous FTP, as shown below.

```
# ftp samba.anu.edu.au
ftp> cd pub/samba
ftp> bin
ftp> get samba-latest.tar.gz
ftp> bye
```

3.  **Unpack the Samba software distribution.**

```
# gnuzip -d -c samba-latest.tar.gz | tar xfv -
```

4.  **Compile the Samba software.**
    Edit the makefile and enable the Solaris-specific configuration, then run
    the command to compile the software.

```
# make BASEDIR=/opt/samba MANDIR=/opt/samba/man
```

This command compiles Samba with /opt/samba as the default
installation base directory, and it installs the binaries here also. If you
want to install Samba in a different directory, you can specify an alternate
BASEDIR directory.

**Configuring Samba**

The Samba software can be run as a standalone server using either the startup
scripts in the /etc/init.d directory, or it can be run using the inetd service.
Preferably, the Samba server should be run using the inetd service, so the server
is initiated only upon a client request. This method makes better use of server
resources.

1.  **Add the following entries to the /etc/services database, or the appro-
    priate name service map if you are using either NIS or NIS+.**

```
netbios-ssn    139/tcp
netbios-ns     137/udp
```

**2.**    **Add the following entries to the** /etc/inetd.conf **file.**

```
netbios-ssn stream tcp nowait root /opt/samba/bin/smbd smbd
netbios-ns dgram udp wait root /opt/samba/bin/nmbd nmbd
```

The smbd daemon provides file access and printer services for Windows LAN Manager clients using the SMB protocol. An SMB session is created upon a client request, and each client receives a separate invocation of the daemon for each session. This daemon then services all connections made by the client during that session. When all the client connections are closed, the daemon for that client terminates.

The nmbd daemon provides name server support to Windows clients. It understands and replies to the netbios name service requests generated by the Windows LAN Manager clients. It also enables resource browsing on the Windows clients using the Microsoft Network Neighborhood, and similar network browsing applications. When a Windows LAN Manager client starts up, it may wish to automatically locate a LAN Manager server, and the nmbd daemon simply listens and responds to such requests.

### Configuring Samba

Next, you need to create a configuration file that defines how Windows clients access Solaris server resources. The configuration is used for the following purposes:

- Establish access policies

- Specify the access log file

- Specify access logging level

- Enable encrypted passwords

- Define access to existing UNIX printers using symbolic names

- Define network interfaces

You can find sample configuration files in the example directories provided with the Samba distribution. Copy one of the sample files from the examples/simple/smb.conf directory to the /opt/samba/lib directory and edit it appropriately. We'll describe some of the common configurations that you may want to enable.

### Home Directory Access

You can map Solaris user login names into the LAN Manager name space to enable Windows users to access their home directories using a UNC path name similar to the following.

```
\\smb-server\\Solaris-login
```

To enable this functionality, insert the following entries into the smb.conf file.

```
[home]
    comment = Home Directories
    browseable = no
    read only = no
    create mode = 0755
```

### File System Access

You can also specify the UFS file system to be shared with Windows clients. In this example, the /art/common file system is specified as a file sharing resource in the smb.conf file.

```
[common]
        comment = /art/common
        path = /art/common
        writable = no
        public = yes
```

### *Configuring the Windows Client*

After Samba services are configured on the server, any Windows clients on the network can view the Solaris server as a Windows file server and/or print server. When a Windows 95 or Windows NT user browses the Network Neighborhood, the Solaris server configured with the Samba software appears as a Windows file server.

Only the exported directories specified in the smbd.conf file on the Solaris server are accessible. Users can easily access these directories by using the Microsoft Explorer to map network drives using UNC path names, such as \\server\directory. Users can also map the network drive manually using the net command in a DOS window, as shown in the following example.

```
C:> net use Z:\\server\directory
```

In this section, we'll describe how to configure the Windows client using Microsoft Explorer.

1. **Double-click the Microsoft Explorer icon.**
2. **Select Tools ➤ Find ➤ Computer.**
   An example is shown below.

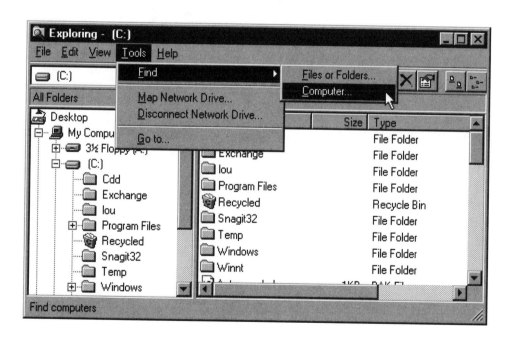

The Find Computer window is displayed.

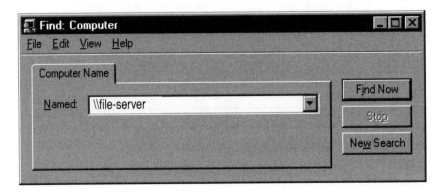

3. **Type the file server host name in the Computer Name field and click the Find Now button.**

   The file server appears as a Windows 95 PC using LAN Manager. This is enabled by the Samba software running on the Solaris server.

4. **Select Tools ➤ Map Network Drive in the Explorer window.**

   An example is shown as follows.

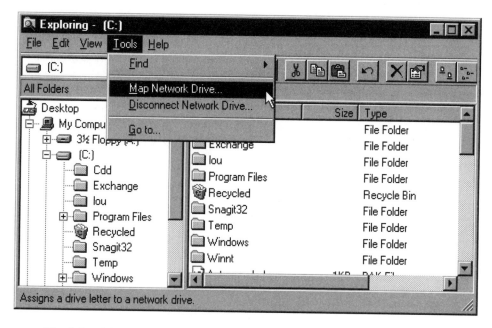

The Map Network Drive window is displayed.

**5.    Select an open drive, type in** \\file-server\common\art, **and click the OK button.**

An example is shown below.

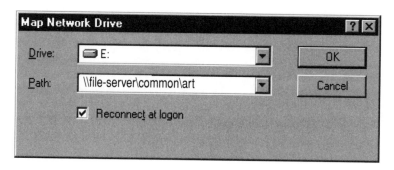

This enables the user to browse the file server using Microsoft Explorer. Complete this step, and you're done.

## Summary

A file sharing service is an integral intranet component, and the NFS file sharing protocol has proven to be a viable solution for an intranet. In this chapter, we've described how to use Samba to extend native Solaris file sharing capabilities to support a heterogenous file sharing environment that includes Windows clients. Samba is a convenient way to enable access to UFS file systems from the Windows desktop. It eliminates the need to install specialized networking software on every Windows desktop to provide access to centralized data, which results in a huge cost savings in desktop maintenance. Also, efforts are under way to standardize the set of programs used in Samba into a common internet file system, also known as CIFS.

Though this file sharing configuration is suitable for many intranets, it may not meet your requirements, particularly in the areas of performance and ease-of-administration. An interesting industry trend is the use of specialized, single-purpose network devices that perform a particular task exceptionally well. For example, several vendors[6] offer dedicated network devices that provide multi-protocol file sharing services, including NFS and the Windows file sharing protocol, while others[7] support NFS only. These devices are extremely easy to set up and use, and they provide higher levels of service and performance.

---

6.   For more information, visit http://www.netapp.com/.
7.   For more information, visit http://www.sun.com/products-n-solutions/hw/servers/netra/netra_nfs/ and http://www.auspex.com/.

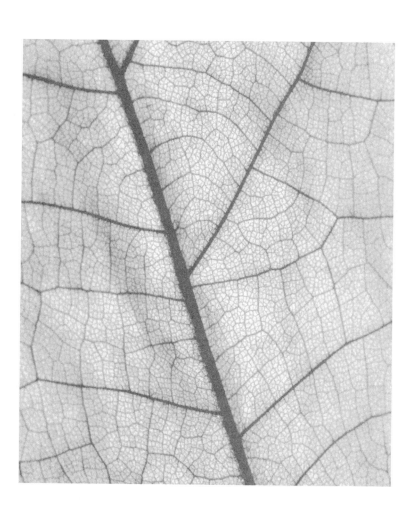

# CHAPTER 11

# Name Services

A name service, also known as a directory service, enables the location independence of intranet resources and gives users a single, logical view of the intranet. An example name service is NIS, Sun's network information service. In this chapter, we'll discuss name services available in Solaris and Windows.

## What is a Name Service?

A name service provides an easy-to-use, unified convention for naming computing resources within and across an intranet. For example, you can organize user and group information using a name service, and enable the global identification of users and groups from anywhere in the intranet. Name service information that is shared by a group of hosts in an intranet is called a *domain*.

Here are some of the benefits a name service brings to the intranet:

- Centralized administration
- No identity conflicts

  For example, users are uniquely identified within a domain.

- Users easily associate resources with names in a consistent manner
- Physical resources associated with names are reassigned without affecting service to users
- Easy user account administration

You can easily administer user accounts and set policies for users based on their needs. At the same time, users can customize their environment.

Without the benefit of a name service, many administration tasks must be performed individually on each desktop computer. In a corporate intranet that is potentially comprised of thousand of systems, this is a difficult and expensive undertaking—hence the need for name services.

## Resource Management Using Name Services

Using name services, you can map a logical name to an intranet resource that describes the resource. For example, you can map the name `mailer` to the IP address of the server system that stores and forward e-mail messages. Similarly, you can also map names to other resources that provide intranet services. Here are other intranet resources that can be managed using a name service:

- File servers
- Print servers
- Mail servers
- News servers
- Time servers

In the Solaris, resource mapping information is stored in several network maps. For example, the `hosts` network map is used to map logical host names to IP addresses:

```
129.145.221.9   mailhost
```

The advantage of using logical names is that users don't have to remember difficult host names or IP addresses to access intranet resources. By assigning simple, straightforward names to the servers that provide the resources, you enable easy access for users.

### Aliases

A logical name may be aliased to a different host in each domain. As the user moves within a corporate intranet from one domain to another, the name used to access an important resource such as a file sharing service remains the same.

Here are examples of using aliases for commonly-used intranet resources:

- `/usr/local`

  This is the directory location for files that are provided using a file sharing service.

- `mailhost`

  This alias is used by mail services to find the host where e-mail is deposited for later retrieval.

- `newshost`

  This alias is used by a network news reader application to establish a network connection to the news server.

Aliases are an example of how a name service allows flexibility and ease of administration. If you decide to change or relocate the system that hosts an intranet resource, you can do so in a manner that is transparent to end-users with minimal disruption of the service by simply updating the record in the name service.

## Name Services

The name services available in a modern operating system environment such as Solaris provide you with capabilities similar to a centralized database to store resource mapping information. Clients of the name service communicate over the network to the name server, where the resource mapping database is stored. A *name space* is a global naming scheme across networked computing resources. A consistent name space can be applied to user, hosts, and other intranet resources.

### Solaris Name Space

To access intranet resources, a host running Solaris uses files residing in the local `/etc` directory, or the host uses a name service such as NIS or NIS+. Here are some examples of the name service databases used in Solaris:

- `services`

  Database that maps network services to port numbers and protocols.

- `passwd`

  Database that stores user login, UID, home directory, and other related information.

- `hosts`

  Database that maps host name to IP addresses.

### Windows Name Space

The Windows system registry is used to store machine-specific information. The registry resides on the local file system for each machine. It acts as a repository for user, host, and network-specific resources.

The Solaris and Windows name space differences are described in Table 11-1.

**Table 11-1** Solaris and Windows Name Services Differences

| Information Type | Solaris Location(s) | Windows System Registry Location |
|---|---|---|
| User Preferences | Home Directory | HU[1]/Default |
| Host Information | /etc Directory, Name service | HLM[2]/System |
| Network Information | /etc Directory, Name service | HLM/Software/Microsoft/Window NT/current version |

[1]HKEY-USERS
[2]Hardware Local Machine

## Fixed Name Spaces

A fixed name space can be mapped to different shared file resources. A fixed name space is easy for users to remember, and it can be used consistently throughout the intranet.

Fixed name spaces offer the following benefits:

- The search path for users is consistent throughout the intranet.

- Users have a common view of network resources.

- Users access resources using an easy-to-remember name space.

- You can take a network resource off-line for maintenance with minimal disruption of service to users.

Introduce fixed name spaces incrementally. A workgroup-sized intranet may not benefit from a fixed name space, but as the organization grows, access to shared file resources can be better managed by using a fixed name space. Managing a fixed name space avoids the complication and difficulties users can have accessing unorganized network resources.

### Solaris AutoFS

AutoFS is a fixed name space that enables users to access file services using a consistent hierarchical method. Similar to other name services, AutoFS maps NFS file sharing resources to logical names. With AutoFS, users access file sharing resources within the domain by using a single name space, /net.

For example, the shared file systems on a file server are easily displayed using the following command.

```
% ls /net/file-server
export opt usr var
```

Besides the special /net name space, you can also create a fixed name space by using an AutoFS direct map, as shown in the following example.

```
/usr/local      file-server:/export/apps
```

The fixed name can be mapped to several servers, improving availability of shared file resources, as shown below.

```
/usr/local      file-serverA:/export/dist
                file-serverB:/export/apps
```

A client that uses this AutoFS map sends a null NFS packet to each file server listed in the map. The first server that responds is theoretically the least-loaded server, and AutoFS mounts the server automatically for the client. If the file server becomes unavailable after the client mounts it, then the client will attempt to "fail-over" to the next available server if the client is running the Solaris 2.6 operating environment. If the client is running an earlier release of Solaris, no fail-over attempt is made, and the client must wait until the server is available.

### Windows Universal Naming Code (UNC)

The Windows environment enables users to access file sharing resources using the UNC path, as shown in the following example.

```
\\machine-name\exported-directory
```

This naming scheme does not support mapping multiple server resources to a fixed name space. If the server referenced in the UNC path is unavailable, users cannot access an alternate host and must wait until the server becomes available.

Though a file sharing naming scheme similar to AutoFS is not available in Windows, file systems accessed using a drive letter can be mapped to an exported directory on the Windows desktop. Users can also access shared file resources within the domain by using a common naming scheme.

```
\\machine-name\exported-directory
```

The Windows Network Neighborhood is a graphical user interface that enables users to browse shared file resources within the domain. This is similar to the /net functionality available in Solaris AutoFS.

## Personal Name Spaces

To augment a centrally managed name space, users have the ability to manage a *personal name space*. A personal name space is a name space that is managed entirely by the user. The user chooses the names of the aliases to map to resources, and they can delete and rename these mappings at will, without affecting anyone else.

### Solaris Symbolic Links

Solaris enables users to manage their personal name space by creating links. A link is a file that points to another item such as a file, application, directory, or other resource. Because the links are created and controlled by users, they can name the link using whatever name that makes sense to them. The following example shows the commands a user types in to create a link to a shared resource, such as a shared directory that contains application executable files.

```
% ln -s /file-server/usr/local apps
```

After creating this link, the user accesses applications by using the path name `apps`. The user doesn't have to remember the longer path name to access the resource, and access is simplified.

### Solaris Shell Startup Files

The `.cshrc` shell startup file can include *aliases* to commonly used resources that employ a fixed name space. An alias is a file that points to another item such as a file, application, directory, or device. For example, an application such as FrameMaker can be aliased using a fixed name space:

```
alias maker '/usr/local/bin/maker'
```

In this example, the `/usr/local` pathname is a fixed name space that is managed.

You can maintain a consistent name space for users by setting up the user's search path using the `.cshrc` or `.profile` startup files so that the user accesses commands, applications, and files using a fixed name space.

### Windows Shortcuts

A shortcut is a Windows feature that is similar to an alias. It enables users to create shortcuts to commonly used files, applications, and other resources. Because the shortcuts are created and controlled by users, they use whatever name that makes sense to them for the shortcut.

## Summary

Name services enable intranet users to easily access important intranet resources, such as file servers and e-mail servers. As an intranet administrator, name services provide you with a powerful method to manage the access to intranet resources, without having to administer every desktop individually. In the next chapter, we'll describe how to set up a name service that is commonly used in many intranets, the Domain Name Service (DNS).

# CHAPTER
# 12

# Setting Up Domain Name Services

The Domain Name Service[1] (DNS) is a *name service*. A name service works much in the way we use an operator to provide us with the phone number to a party we want to call using the telephone. We know the name of the party we want to call, but lacking the phone number to dial, we turn to a reliable third party to provide us with the additional information we need. In a similar fashion, a name service works within an intranet to provide user, host, network, and other types of information needed to perform common intranet activities such as printing, web browsing, sending e-mail, and so on. Without a name service, we would be forced to use long and difficult-to-remember IP addresses each time we wanted to print a file, or browse a web site — certainly not a desirable activity.

Name services match a key, which is a parameter provided by the requestor (a user, a host, a process, and so on), to a value. For example, a host name is a key that is mapped to an associated value, an IP address. The activity of finding values for keys on behalf of a requestor is called *resolution*. Properly configured, a name service is unobtrusive, and works quietly and reliably behind the scenes. In this chapter, we'll look at DNS, a name service used in the Internet and intranet to resolve host names to IP addresses.

---

1.  For more information, visit http://www.internic.net/rfc/rfc1034.txt/.

## Host Name Resolution

To explain how host name resolution works, we'll use the scenario where we have two networked systems and we need to establish a connection between the two, as shown in Figure 12-1.

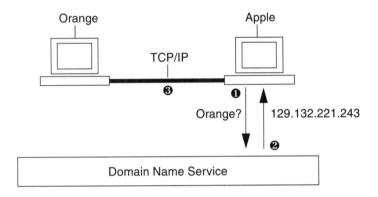

**Figure 12-1** DNS Host Name Resolution

In order for apple to connect to orange using the network, apple needs to obtain orange's 32-bit Internet Protocol (IP) address. To obtain the address, apple uses DNS, a global facility for dynamically resolving machine names to IP addresses. Similar to NIS or NIS+, DNS enables the resolution of machines names in an intranet to their IP addresses.

## DNS Name Space

The DNS name space is the sum total of all the TCP/IP addresses used in the Internet. As you can imagine, there are millions of systems on the Internet, and no single database can hold all the entries and keep them up-to-date. Potentially, the same problem can arise in an intranet. To address this problem, DNS uses a distributed database facility that delegates the responsibility of maintaining IP addresses to the local authority for discrete portions of the network known as *domains*. Fortunately, this distributed model also works very well in an intranet, and DNS services can easily be scaled to accomodate growth.

### DNS Domains

DNS domains are organized hierarchically in the Internet. The first tier of the Internet name space, also known as the *top-level* domain, is shown in Figure 12-2.

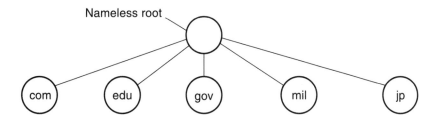

**Figure 12-2** Internet DNS Top-Level Domain

Top-level domains are administered by the Network Information Center (NIC). Domains that fall below the top-level domain are called sub-domains, as shown in Figure 12-3.

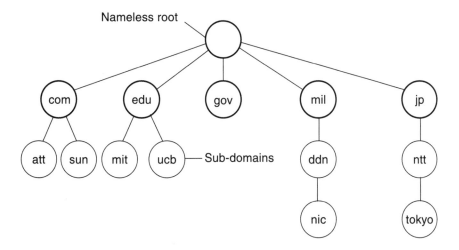

**Figure 12-3** Internet DNS Top-Level and Sub-Domains

The administration of these domains is delegated to the companies, organizations, and other groups that are registered as authorities for each sub-domain. In a similar manner, the administration of host name and IP address information can be distributed to groups across an intranet, enabling flexible and decentralized management.

### DNS Domain Names

DNS domains use a unique identifier called the domain name. The domain name is made up of labels separated by periods that reflect the location of the domain in the DNS name space, as shown in this example.

---

sun.com.
hq.nasa.gov

---

A domain name that ends with a period is called an absolute or *fully-qualified* domain name (FQDN), as shown in this example.

---

widget.central.company.com.

---

Domain names that do not end with a period are called relative or *partially-qualified domain names* (PQDN), as shown below.

---

widget.central

---

### *DNS Domains in the Intranet*

The DNS name space of an intranet can be organized logically in a number of ways, such as by business function, as shown in Figure 12-4.

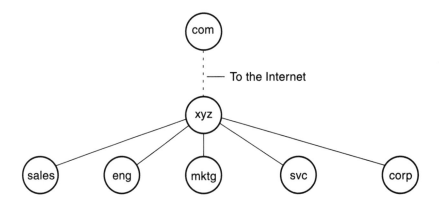

**Figure 12-4** Example – Intranet DNS Name Space by Function

An intranet DNS name space organization by geography is shown in Figure 12-5.

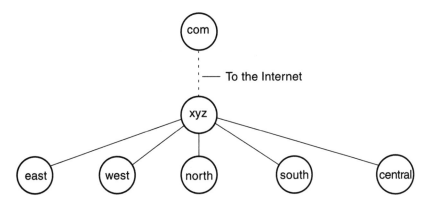

**Figure 12-5** Example – Intranet DNS Name Space by Geography

### DNS Zone of Authority

A DNS zone of authority describes the portions of the name space where host records are managed. A zone of authority can map to a single domain in the name space, or it can span multiple domains.

For example, the host information (IP addresses) of the domains solaris.sales.xyz.com and java.eng.xyz.com are managed by the host dnsserver.xyz.com., as shown in Figure 12-6.

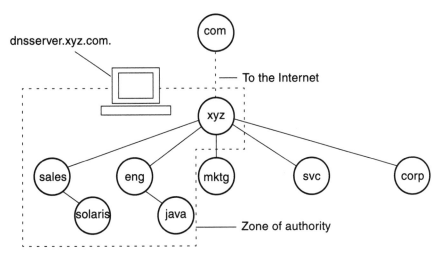

**Figure 12-6** Example – DNS Zone of Authority

The host `dnsserver.xyz.com.` is the DNS authority for the domains `solaris.sales.xyz.com` and `java.eng.xyz.com`. Any host that wants to resolve the address for the sub-domain `solaris.sales.xyz.com` contacts `dnsserver.xyz.com` for host name resolution.

## Acquiring a DNS Domain Name

The InterNIC[2] is the organization to contact to register domains, obtain IP network numbers, and so on. Setting up DNS in an intranet also includes registering with InterNIC. By registering your name space, you can control the sub-domains within your DNS domain.

## DNS Servers

Several types of DNS servers can be used to manage host information within the name space, as described in Table 12-1.

**Table 12-1** DNS Server Types

| DNS Server Type | Description |
|---|---|
| `Primary DNS Server` | The zone authority for host information. Hostnames and IP addresses are stored and maintained on this server. It can also update other DNS servers within the zone of authority, and assign hostname resolution authority for sub-domains to other DNS servers. |
| `Secondary DNS Server` | Stores copies of the host information on the primary server. Can take over if primary is unavailable, and can help distribute hostname resolution workload in busy networks. |
| `Caching DNS Server` | Keeps a copy of recently used DNS information for quick reuse in a specified time period. Also known as a "non-authoritative server." |
| `DNS Root Servers` | The servers designated by the NIC to act as authorities for the top levels of the DNS name space. Primary servers must be configured to use these servers for "top-down" resolution. |

---

2.   Visit the InterNIC Web site at http://rs0.internic.net/. This site provides you with all the information you need to register your DNS domain.

Generally speaking, secondary and caching DNS servers improve the performance of DNS hostname resolution in large, busy networks. Though useful in these types of environments, they are not required to implement DNS, unlike a primary DNS server.

### Authoritative and Non-Authoritative DNS Servers

As indicated in Table 12-1, an authoritative server is a primary DNS server that is the zone authority for host information. In some cases, host name resolution can be performed more quickly and easily by using a caching DNS server, or a non-authoritative server. The non-authoritative DNS server stores recently requested IP address information in a local cache. The non-authoritative DNS server associates a time-to-live (TTL) value with cached data to determine how long the information is valid. Subsequently, if a client requests to resolve a host name, the IP address is provided by the non-authoritative server if the TTL has not expired, eliminating the need to traverse the network to obtain the information from the authoritative server.

This capability also helps distribute the load among DNS servers, and promotes a decentralized environment where no single DNS server must be consulted for host name resolution. Non-authoritative DNS servers also help improve DNS service availability since they provide IP address resolution when the primary DNS server is unavailable or unreachable due to a failure in the network.

### Primary DNS Server Components

A primary DNS server consists of the following:

*   DNS server process

    This process is the DNS server that runs on a host. In UNIX environments, the process is typically called `in.named`. Similar DNS server functionality is available for Windows NT.

*   DNS configuration files

    These files are used to bootstrap the DNS server process.

*   A local database

    This text file describes IP address to host name mapping for machines within the DNS domain.

## DNS Aliases

A DNS alias enables you to map more than one host name to an IP address. For example, you can map a host serving a web site to a particular IP address using an alias:

```
129.152.221.11        www.site.com web-server
```

Client systems use the alias to access the web site, and not the IP address, This enables flexibility as the web site changes. For example, if you decide to move the web site to a more powerful server later, you can simply change the IP address the alias is mapped to. Clients will automatically use the new web server without any disruption in service because they access the site using the alias, and not the actual IP address.

### Aliasing Services with DNS

DNS aliases provide the flexibility to remap intranet services to different physical machines without having to change client configurations or alert users to changes. In this example, the host name of a machine that provides e-mail services is mapped to an IP address.

```
129.152.221.10        mailhost mailhost.xyz.company.com
```

By using an alias to map a service such as e-mail, you can move the e-mail services from one physical machine to another, and simply update the DNS alias to effect the change for all the clients. You can change the IP address of `mailhost` without having to worry about mail being forwarded to the wrong destination. You don't have to touch individual configurations on each of the clients, improving the reliability of the service and reducing administration.

## DNS Resolvers

DNS resolving is when a client system queries a DNS server with a hostname to obtain an IP address. A DNS resolver is the software that enables this capability.

### Solaris DNS Resolver

On Solaris systems, the DNS resolver is implemented as a dynamically loaded library named `/usr/lib/libsocket.a`. This library is called by programs using the `gethostbyname(3N)` function. The resolver can also be called explicitly, using the `nslookup` command. No client-side DNS process is necessary.

### Windows DNS Resolver

A dynamically loadable library (DLL) named `winsock.dll`[3] is used to implement DNS resolution in Windows. The DLL is stored in the `C:/windows` directory, and performs DNS lookups like the `gethostbyname(3N)` function in Solaris. This DLL also performs many of the other TCP functions found in the Solaris `libsocket.a` library.

## Setting Up DNS Services

This section provides an overview of the tasks required to set up Solaris-based DNS services. We'll set up DNS services using the following scenario:

- DNS server types: root and primary (sub-domain) DNS servers

- DNS server OS: Solaris

- DNS server host names: `root-dns`, `sales-dns`

- Domains: root (`.`), `sales`

- DNS client types: Solaris and Windows 95

The topology for our scenario is described in Figure 12-7.

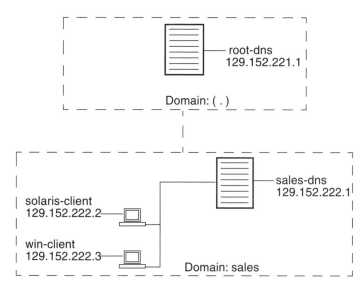

**Figure 12-7** DNS Scenario Topology

---

3. For more information, visit http://www.intel.com/IAL/winsock2/.

### Task Prerequisites

- Register the domain name and request a block of IP addresses.

- Determine the DNS domain hierarchy.

### Task Overview

- Create the files and directories used for DNS services on the servers.

- Configure the servers to provide DNS services after a system reboot.

- Test and verify DNS services.

- Set up the client systems to use DNS services.

### Configuring the Root DNS Server

To configure the root DNS server, we'll create the following configuration files and populate them with entries required by DNS.

- `named.boot`

  Bootstraps the DNS server process.

- `cache`

  Contains the root DNS server host name and IP address.

- `root.rzone`

  Contains reversed-IP addresses for the domain.

- `root.zone`

  Contains DNS server, host name, and IP address information for the domain.

- `loopback`

  Describes the DNS start of authority.

- `nsswitch.conf`

  The name service switch file, used in Solaris to establish the policy for host name resolution.

In this section, we'll describe the entries that must appear in each file.

1. **Log into the server as root.**

2. **Create the** `named` **directory.**
   This is the directory where the DNS configuration files are stored.

```
# mkdir /etc/named
```

3. **Create the** `named.boot` **file.**
   The `named.boot` file is read by the DNS server process `in.named`(1M) at startup time. It bootstraps the server with initial DNS configuration information.

```
# touch /etc/named.boot
```

**4.** **Add the entries specified in Example 12-1 to the** `named.boot` **file.**

**Example 12-1** Root DNS Server `named.boot` File

```
;
; DNS (in.named) boot file for the root server
;
;type       domain  source file or host
;-----------------------------------------------------------------
❶ DIRECTORY  /etc/named
❷ CACHE         .       cache
❸ PRIMARY    IN-ADDR.ARPA     root.rzone
❹ PRIMARY       .       root.zone
❺ PRIMARY    0.0.127.IN-ADDR.ARPA         loop.back
```

The entries in this file are described below.

❶ Specifies the directory location of the DNS configuration files.

❷ Specifies the file containing the root DNS server host name and IP address.

❸ Specifies the file containing reversed-IP addresses for the domain.

❹ Specifies the file containing DNS server, host name, and IP address information for the domain.

❺ Specifies the file describing the DNS start of authority.

**5.** **Create the** `cache` **file, and add the entries shown below.**

**Example 12-2** Root DNS Server `cache` File

```
;
; /etc/named/cache file for the root (.) domain server
;
;
;


.        IN NS    root-dns
root-dns    IN A    129.152.221.1
```

**6.**  **Create the** `root.rzone` **file, and add the entries shown in Example 12-3.**

**Example 12-3** Root DNS Server `root.rzone` File

```
;
; /etc/named/root.rzone file for the root (.) nameserver
;


$ORIGIN     IN-ADDR.ARPA.

❶ IN-ADDR.ARPA.   IN SOA  root-dns. root.root-dns. (
           0000.0000   ; version number
           10800       ; refresh (3hrs)
           3600        ; retry (1hr)
           432000      ; expire (5days)
           86400 )     ; minimum (1day)


  IN-ADDR.ARPA.   IN NS   root-dns.

 ; Example entry:     reversed-IP-address   IN   PTR   host-name.

❷ 1.221.152.129  IN PTR root-dns.

 ; Example entry:     reversed-IP-net-address   IN   PTR   host-name.domain.

❸ 222.152.129   IN NS   sales-dns.sales.

 ; Example entry:     reversed-IP-address   IN   PTR   host-name.domain.

❹ 1.222.152.129  IN PTR sales-dns.sales.
```

The entries in this file are described below.

❶  Specifies the `IN-ADDR.ARPA.` values for the DNS server.

❷  The reversed IP address entry for the root ( . ) DNS server. If there are any clients in the ( . ) domain, enter these here.

❸  The reversed IP *network* address entry for the DNS sub-domain server.

❹  The reversed IP address entry for the DNS sub-domain server.

7.   Create the `root.zone` **file, and add the entries shown in Example 12-4.**

**Example 12-4** Root DNS Server `root.zone` File

```
;
; /etc/named/root.zone file for the root (.) nameserver
;


$ORIGIN .


;
; Start of Authority section
;

❶ .         IN SOA root-dns. root.root-dns. (
           0000.0000    ; version number
           10800        ; refresh (3hrs.)
           3600         ; retry (1hr.)
           432000       ; expire (5days)
           86400 )      ; minimum (1day)
;
; Domain Nameserver Section
;

❷ .         IN NS root-dns.
  sales.    IN NS sales-dns.sales.


;
; Host Information section
;

❸ localhost         IN A    127.0.0.1
  root-dns          IN A    129.152.221.1
  sales-dns.sales.  IN A    129.152.222.1
```

The entries in this file are described below.

   ❶   Specifies the Start of Authority (SOA) values for the DNS server.

   ❷   Specifies the domain name servers.

   ❸   Specifies the domain name server IP addresses.

**8.** Create the `loop.back` file, and add the entries shown below.

**Example 12-5** Root DNS Server `loop.back` File

```
;
; /etc/named/loop.back file for the root (.) nameserver
;


;
; Start of Authority section
;

$ORIGIN  0.0.127.IN-ADDR.ARPA.

0.0.127.IN-ADDR.ARPA.    IN SOA root-dns. root.root-dns. (
        0000.0000    ; version number
        10800        ; refresh (3hrs.)
        3600         ; retry (1hr.)
        432000       ; expire (5days)
        86400 )      ; minimum (1day)

0.0.127.IN-ADDR.ARPA.    IN NS  root-dns.
1            IN PTR localhost.
```

**9.** Edit the `/etc/nsswitch.conf` file, and verify that the `hosts` entry appears as follows.

```
hosts:        files dns
```

Complete this step, and you're done configuring the root DNS server. Next, configure the sub-domain DNS server.

### Configuring the Sub-Domain DNS Server

The configuration process for the sub-domain DNS server is very similar to configuring a root DNS server. To configure the sub-domain DNS server, we'll create the following configuration files and populate them with entries required by DNS.

- `named.boot`

  Bootstraps the DNS server process.

- `cache`

  Contains the root DNS server host name and IP address.

- `sales.rzone`

  Contains reversed-IP addresses for the domain.

- `sales.zone`

  Contains DNS server, host name, and IP address information for the domain.

- `loopback`

  Describes the DNS start of authority.

- `nsswitch.conf`

  The name service switch file, used in Solaris to establish the policy for host name resolution.

In this section, we'll describe the entries that must appear in each file.

1.  **Log into the server as root.**

2.  **Create the** `named` **directory.**
    This is the directory where the DNS configuration files are stored.

```
# mkdir /etc/named
```

3.  **Create the** `named.boot` **file.**
    The `named.boot` file is read by the DNS server process `in.named`(1M) at startup time. It bootstraps the server with initial DNS configuration information.

```
# touch /etc/named.boot
```

**4.**    **Add the entries specified in Example 12-6 to the** `named.boot` **file.**

**Example 12-6** Sub-Domain DNS Server `named.boot` File

```
;
; DNS (in.named) boot file for the sub domain server
;
;type        domain   source file or host
;------------------------------------------------------------------
❶ DIRECTORY    /etc/named
❷ CACHE        .        cache
❸ PRIMARY      sales    sales.zone
❹ PRIMARY      222.152.129.IN-ADDR.ARPA      sales.rzone
❺ PRIMARY      0.0.127.IN-ADDR.ARPA       loop.back
```

The entries in this file are described below.

❶    Specifies the directory location of the DNS configuration files.

❷    Specifies the file containing the root DNS server host name and IP address.

❸    Specifies the file containing DNS server, host name, and IP address information for the domain.

❹    Specifies the file containing reversed-IP addresses for the domain.

❺    Specifies the file describing the DNS start of authority.

**5.**    **Create the** `cache` **file, and add the entries shown below.**

**Example 12-7** Sub-Domain DNS Server `cache` File

```
;
; /etc/named/cache file containing the name and address
; of the root (.) name server
;

.         IN NS    root-dns.
root-dns.     IN A     129.152.221.1
```

**6.**   Create the `sales.zone` file, and add the entries shown in Example 12-8.

**Example 12-8** Sub-Domain DNS Server `sales.zone` File

```
;
; /etc/named/sales.zone file for the sales (sales.)
; sub domain nameserver
;


$ORIGIN sales.


;
; Start of Authority section
;

❶ sales.        IN SOA dns-sales.sales. root.sale-dns.sales. (
        0000.0000    ; version number
        10800        ; refresh (3hrs.)
        3600         ; retry (1hr.)
        432000       ; expire (5days)
        86400 )      ; minimum (1day)

;
; Domain Section
;

❷ sales.        IN NS sales-dns.sales.


;
; Host Information section
;

❸ localhost.         IN A     127.0.0.1
  solaris-client     IN A     129.152.222.2
  win-client         IN A     129.152.222.3
```

The entries in this file are described below.

❶   Specifies the Start of Authority (SOA) values for the DNS server.

❷   Specifies the domain name server.

❸   Specifies the IP addresses of the hosts in the domain.

**7.    Create the** `sales.rzone` **file, and add the entries shown in Example 12-9.**

**Example 12-9** Sub-Domain DNS Server `sales.rzone` File

```
    ;
    ; /etc/named/sales.rzone file for the sales (sales.) nameserver
    ;

    $ORIGIN     222.152.129.IN-ADDR.ARPA.

❶ 222.152.129.IN-ADDR.ARPA.   IN SOA sales-dns.sales. root.sales-dns.dns.
    (
            0000.0000    ; version number
            10800        ; refresh (3hrs)
            3600         ; retry (1hr)
            432000       ; expire (5days)
            86400 )      ; minimum (1day)

❷ 222.152.129.IN-ADDR.ARPA.    IN NS    sales-dns.sales.

    ; Example entry:    host-portion-of-IP-address   IN  PTR  host-name.domain.

❸ 2   IN PTR solaris-client.sales.
    3   IN PTR win-client.sales.
```

The entries in this file are described below.

❶    Specifies the `IN-ADDR.ARPA.` values for the DNS server.

❷    The reversed network IP address entry for the sales (`sales.`) DNS server.

❸    The reversed IP address entry for hosts in the sales (`sales.`) domain. Only the host portion of the IP address is required.

8. Create the `loop.back` file, and add the entries shown below.

**Example 12-10** Sub-Domain DNS Server `loop.back` File

```
;
; /etc/named/loop.back file for the sales (sales.) nameserver
;


;
; Start of Authority section
;

$ORIGIN  0.0.127.IN-ADDR.ARPA.

0.0.127.IN-ADDR.ARPA.   IN SOA sales-dns.sales. root.sales-dns.sales. (
        0000.0000    ; version number
        10800        ; refresh (3hrs.)
        3600         ; retry (1hr.)
        432000       ; expire (5days)
        86400 )      ; minimum (1day)

0.0.127.IN-ADDR.ARPA.   IN NS   sales-dns.sales.
1            IN PTR localhost.
```

9. Edit the `/etc/nsswitch.conf` file, and verify that the `hosts` entry appears as follows.

```
hosts:        files dns
```

Complete this step, and you're done configuring the sub-domain DNS server. Next, start DNS services on each server.

### Starting DNS Services

1.  To start DNS services at system boot time, ensure these entries appear in the `/etc/init.d/inetserver` file.

```
#
# If this machine is configured to be an Internet Domain Name
# System (DNS) server, run the name daemon.
# Start named prior to: route add net host, to avoid dns
# gethostbyname timout delay for nameserver during boot.
#
if [ -f /usr/sbin/in.named -a -f /etc/named.boot ]; then
/usr/sbin/in.named; echo "starting internet domain name server."
fi
```

2.  Reboot the system.

```
# init 6
```

The `inetserver` start up script checks for the `/etc/named.boot` file. If found, the DNS server process is started. By creating the `/etc/named.boot` file, and creating the corresponding files specified in the `/etc/named` directory, the DNS services are started by rebooting the DNS server.

Complete this step, and you're done starting DNS services. Next, verify DNS services on each server.

### Testing and Verifying the DNS Server

Once you have configured and started DNS services, use the `nslookup(1)` command on the newly-configured DNS server to verify that DNS services are available.

In the following example, `nslookup` is used to request the IP address for a specified host name.

```
% nslookup host-name
Server:   dns-server.domain-name
Address:  IP-address

Name:     host-name
Address:  IP-address
```

These results indicate that DNS services are available on the server, and the server has been set up properly.

There are many other capabilities provided by `nslookup`. To give you an idea of its usefulness as a troubleshooting tool, we'll provide you with several examples.

You can also use `nslookup` in interactive mode, as shown below.

```
% nslookup
Default Server:  dns-server.domain-name
Address:  IP-address
```

By default, the FQDN and the IP address of the DNS server is displayed. To display all the commands available for nslookup, type a ? character, as shown in this example.

```
> nslookup ?
nslookup query options
. . .
```

To find the DNS servers for a domain, use the ls command. In this example, the root-level DNS servers are displayed.

```
> ls .
[dns-server.domain-name]
  (root).                    server = dns-server.domain-name
  dns-server2.domain-name2   IP-address
  (root).                    server = dns-server.domain-name
  dns-server3.domain-name3   IP-address
. . .
```

You can also  print a full listing of all the host names and IP addresses for a DNS domain, as shown below.

```
> ls company.com
[dns-server.company.COM]
  company.COM.               server = dns-server.company.COM
  dns-server.company.COM     IP-address
  host-name1                 IP-address
  host-name2                 IP-address
. . .
```

To verify DNS servers other than the default server, you can use the `server` command, as shown in this example.

```
> server dns-server.other.company.COM
Default Server:  dns-server.other.company.COM
Addresses:  IP-address, IP-address
Aliases:  dns-server.other.company.COM
```

Now, all queries you issue with `nslookup` are resolved by the specified server — a handy feature in case you need to resolve an IP address using an authoritative server.

### Setting Up the Client Systems to Use DNS

Fortunately, the client-side DNS setup is minimal, and all that is required is to configure each DNS client with the appropriate DNS domain name and server addresses, if there are multiple servers providing DNS services in the domain.

### Solaris DNS Client Configuration

1. **Log in as root.**

2. **Edit the** `/etc/nsswitch.conf` **file.**

   The name service switch file is used to set the policy for name service look-ups. It is required since Solaris clients can use multiple name services besides DNS to perform host name resolution. Verify that the `dns` keyword is specified in the search path for the `hosts` entry. If you intend to use DNS as the primary IP address resolver, then the order of the keywords should appear as follows.

   ```
   hosts:  dns files
   ```

3. **Set up the** `/etc/resolv.conf` **file.**

   This file contains the DNS domain name and list of DNS servers. The format is shown below.

   ```
   domain        domain-name
   nameserver    IP-address
   nameserver    IP-address
   ```

The order of the `nameserver` entries matters—the client will query the first server indicated, and it will consult secondary servers only if the first is unavailable.

Complete this step, and you're done.

### Windows DNS Client Configuration

Windows clients interoperate seamlessly with DNS services provided by a Solaris server. Each desktop system is configured in the "Properties" section of the "Network Neighborhood" for the primary network interface.

1.  **Select Control Panel ➤ Network ➤ Configuration.**
    The Configuration window is displayed.

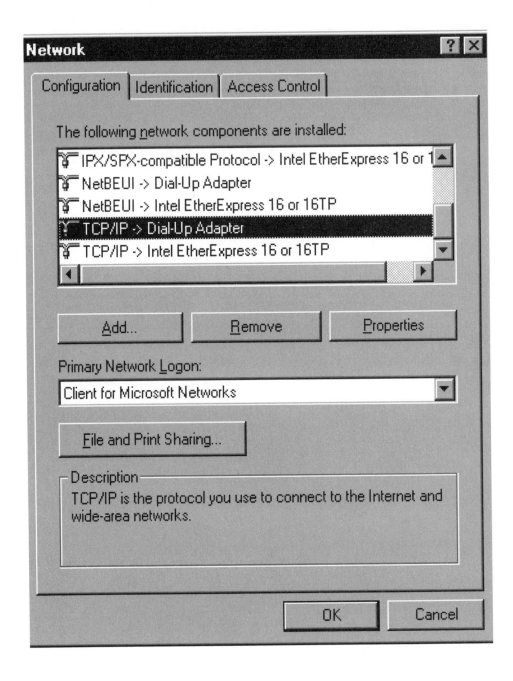

**2.** **Double-click the primary network interface.**
The TCP/IP Properties window is displayed.

**3.** **Click on the DNS Configuration tab in the TCP/IP Properties window.**
The DNS Configuration window is displayed.

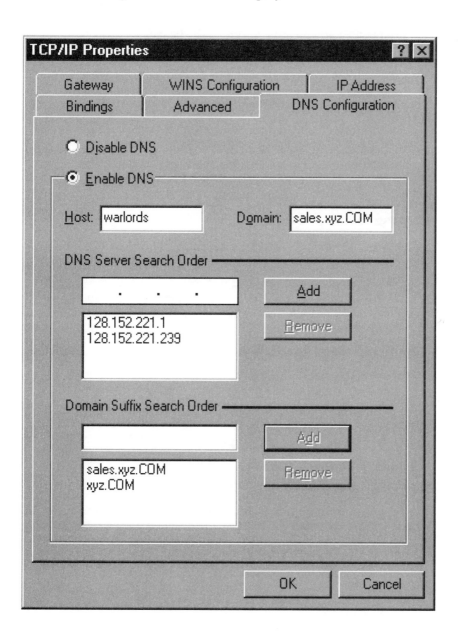

**4.  Fill in the fields with the DNS configuration information.**

The fields shown in this window are described below:

- Host

    This is the host name assigned to the client.

- Domain

    The FQDN of which the desktop is a client.

- DNS Server Search Order

    The order in which the client queries DNS servers. The client will query the first server indicated, and it will consult secondary servers only if the first is unavailable.

- Domain Suffix Search Order

    This field is used to indicate the DNS sub-domain hierarchy, and enables the client to use PQDNs to access intranet resources.

Complete this step, and you're done.

## Integrating DNS and NIS

Solaris provides a convenient way to integrate the NIS and NIS+ name services with DNS. With this level of integration, only the NIS master server and any slave servers require DNS configuration. The NIS client systems in an integrated NIS and DNS domain automatically gain DNS lookup services without any additional configuration. In a corporate intranet, this eases DNS administration and saves time spent on maintenance tasks. This section describes how to integrate NIS and DNS services.

### Task Prerequisites

- Set up the NIS master server

- Set up the DNS server (see *Setting Up DNS Services* on page 175).

### Configuring the NIS Server with DNS Support

**1.  Log into the NIS master server as root.**

**2.  Set up the** /etc/resolv.conf **file.**

This file contains the DNS domain name and a list of DNS servers. The format is shown below.

```
domain        domain-name
nameserver    IP-address
nameserver    IP-address
```

**3.** **Edit the NIS configuration file** `/var/yp/Makefile` **and enable DNS forwarding.**

Enable the `-b` variable, as shown below.

```
...
# Set the following variable to "-b" to have NIS servers use the domain name
# resolver for hosts not in the current domain.
#B=-b
B=-b
```

**4.** **Rebuild the NIS maps.**

```
# cd /var/yp
# make
```

**5.** **Verify the** `/etc/nsswitch.conf` **file is set up correctly.**

The name service switch file is used to set the policy for name service lookups. This file is normally pre-configured, and it does not require editing. The correct setting appears as follows.

```
hosts:  nis files
```

**6.** **If the NIS domain uses slave servers, log into each NIS slave server and set up the** `/etc/resolv.conf` **file.**

Use the same DNS settings you specified in Step 2.

Complete this step, and you're done.

## DNS and Mail Services

In addition to providing host name resolution, DNS is also used to specify the mail depository, or a *mail exchanger* for a domain. DNS can be configured to designate a mail receiver on behalf of a collection of desktop computers, or a domain.

To explain how DNS services and e-mail are used together in an intranet, we'll use a scenario. The desktops shown in Figure 12-8 are not configured to receive mail, but we have used a DNS mail exchange (MX) record to specify the server `mailhost.Sales.XYZ.COM` as the mail exchanger for the `Sales.XYZ.COM` domain.

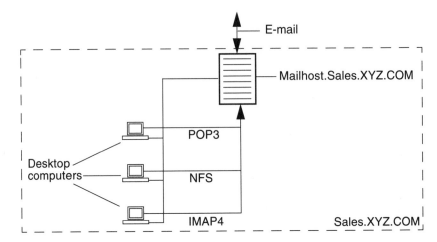

**Figure 12-8** Example – DNS and Mail Service Integration

All e-mail sent to hosts residing in the `Sales.XYZ.COM` domain is received by the server `mailhost.Sales.XYZ.COM`. Desktop clients access e-mail residing on the server using either the POP3, IMAP4, or NFS protocols. This is a desirable e-mail configuration for an intranet desktop, because it provides a secure means of e-mail access. Using a mail host, you can avoid connections from machines outside the domain to desktops inside your domain, which is typical for hosts that reside within a firewall protected intranet.

Another configuration is shown in Figure 12-9, where e-mail intended for intranet desktops is first delivered to a single mail host outside the firewall. The e-mail is later transferred for pickup inside the firewall.

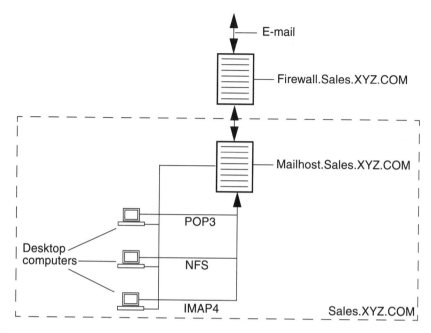

**Figure 12-9** Example – Firewall-Enabled DNS and Mail Service Integration

You can use the nslookup command to determine the mail exchanger for a DNS domain, as shown below.

```
% nslookup -q=mx domain-name dns-server
Server:   dns-server
Address:  IP-address

domain-name        preference = 20, mail exchanger = server1.domain-name
domain-name        preference = 10, mail exchanger = server2.domain-name
domain-name        preference = 30, mail exchanger = server3.domain-name
server1.domain-name      internet address = IP-address
server2.domain-name      internet address = IP-address
server3.domain-name      internet address = IP-address
```

As shown in this example, a DNS domain can use several mail exchangers. Though e-mail is delivered to a single mail exchanger, alternate mail exchangers guarantee the receipt of e-mail in case the primary is unavailable. Priority is used to assign alternate e-mail delivery sites in case the preferred mail exchanger is unavailable. The smaller the preference number, the higher the priority.

## DNS Application Programming Interface (API)

The gethostbyname(3N) system call is used to retrieve information from DNS. This functionality can be useful for custom intranet applications. This system call can be used to perform host name resolution from within a program written in the C or Perl programming languages. The gethostbyname system call uses the FQDN as an argument, and it returns the structure containing all the records associated with the host.

## DNS Reverse-Name Lookups

Earlier, we described the in-addr.arpa address during the DNS setup section. Here, we'll describe how this address is used. DNS supports reverse name lookups. For example, given the IP address, DNS can attempt to resolve the FQDN of that IP address, as shown below.

```
% nslookup
> set querytype=PTR
> 1.9.9.192.in-addr.arpa
> exit
```

Alternately, the same information can be obtained from the command-line interface, as shown below.

```
% nslookup -q=ptr 1.9.9.192.in-addr.arpa
```

Notice the IP addresses should be specified in the reverse order and appended with the special domain of in-addr.arpa.

## Summary

In this chapter, we have provided a basic overview of DNS only. It is likely that you will need additional information to configure DNS services in your intranet, and it is not within the scope of this book to provide detailed DNS set-up and reference information. For more information, consult the system administration documentation that came with your system. Following are additional DNS information sources you may also find useful:

- **DNS and BIND in a Nutshell**, by Paul Albitz, Cricket Liu. Publishers, O'Reilly & Associates. ISBN: 1565920104

- **DNS Related RFCs**
  `http://www.dns.net/dnsrd/docs/rfc.html/`.

- **WEBDNS**
  `http://webdns.lcs.mit.edu/cgi-bin/webdns/about/`.

- **DNS FAQ**
  `http://web.syr.edu/~jmwobus/comfaqs/faq-dns/`.

# CHAPTER 13

# Setting Up
# E-mail Services

E-mail is the primary form of communication for many intranet users. It's a great way to exchange information, since it can overcome the geographical distances that sometimes make communication difficult. It also provides a nice alternative to voice mail and even face-to-face communication, since e-mail can be read when it is most convenient for the recipient to do so, and it can be composed at the sender's convenience also. In this chapter, we'll discuss how e-mail is implemented using the Simple Mail Transfer Protocol (SMTP), the de-facto standard for exchanging e-mail messages. We'll also describe how to set up e-mail services for clients that use the Post Office Protocol (POP) and Interactive Mail Access Protocol (IMAP) protocols, and we'll list the ways in which e-mail services can be extended using e-mail aliases, e-mail filtering, and e-mail forwarding.

## How E-mail Works

The e-mail delivery system is modeled after the postal service. Like a written letter, an e-mail message is delivered to a fixed location (like a mailbox), where it is picked up by the recipient at a convenient time. Just like a piece of postal mail, an e-mail message has these attributes:

- Envelope
- Sender's address
- Recipient's address

- Time of delivery

- Return receipt

### E-mail Components

The e-mail delivery system is a client/server application that uses the following components.

- Mail user agent (MUA)

  This is the client-side application used to send and receive e-mail.

- Mail transfer agent (MTA)

  This is the server-side application that stores and forwards e-mail.

- Mail gateway

  This is a system that facilitates message exchange between mail transfer agents.

To understand how these components interoperate, let's look at what happens when a typical e-mail message is sent. The mail user agent is used to send the e-mail message, then the MTA forwards the message to its destination using intermediaries called *gateways*, where it is deposited in a designated mail storage area. The e-mail message is then delivered to the recipient's mail user agent upon request. Generally, an e-mail message can be routed using several cooperating e-mail gateways until it reaches its destination.

To see how a message was routed, you can examine the mail headers known as the message envelope. Consider Example 13-1.

**Example 13-1** E-mail Message Envelope

```
❹ Received: from Central.Sun.COM (centralmail1.Central.Sun.COM) by
  rmtc.Central.Sun.COM (5.x/SMI-SVR4)
         id AA15725; Thu, 18 Jul 1996 07:00:17 -0600
❸ Received: from mercury.Sun.COM by Central.Sun.COM (SMI-8.6/SMI-5.3)
         id IAA27418; Thu, 18 Jul 1996 08:00:14 -0500
❷ Received: by mercury.Sun.COM (Sun.COM)
         id GAA00632; Thu, 18 Jul 1996 06:00:14 -0700
❶ Received: by dub-img-4.compuserve.com (8.6.10/5.950515)
         id JAA12542; Thu, 18 Jul 1996 09:00:12 -0400
  Message-Id: <960718125707_100765.456_GHV107-1@CompuServe.COM>
```

This e-mail message was sent from a CompuServe user in England and received by the recipient's mail transfer agent located in the Mountain time zone in the U.S. within a few minutes. Below is description of the actions (indicated by the message envelope) required to deliver the message.

❶ The mail gateway `dub-img-4.compuserve.com` routes the message to the next gateway, `mercury.Sun.COM`.

❷ The mail gateway `mercury.Sun.COM` routes the message to the next gateway, `Central.Sun.COM`.

❸ The mail gateway `Central.Sun.COM` delivers the message to the recipient's mail transfer agent, `rmtc.Central.Sun.COM`.

❹ The mail transfer agent `rmtc.Central.Sun.COM` stores the message in the mail spool area for pick up by the recipient's mail user agent.

### E-mail Addresses

E-mail addresses use the user-name@DNS-domain format, as shown below.

---

```
Vasanthan.Dasan@Central.Sun.COM
100765.456@CompuServe.COM
```

---

DNS is described in *Setting Up Domain Name Services* on page 167.

## Using E-mail

There are several e-mail user agent applications available from a number of vendors for both Solaris and Windows. The popular e-mail user agents for the Solaris environment include:

* `mailtool`

    This application uses a GUI and runs in the OpenWindows windowing environment.

* `dtmail`

    This application also uses a GUI, but it runs in the Common Desktop Environment (CDE).

- `mh, elm`

  These e-mail applications use the curses library for formatting character-based displays, and they can be run using a terminal such as a VT-100 or using terminal-emulation software.

- `mail, mailx`

  Both of these e-mail applications run in the Solaris command line interface.

In the Windows environment, the popular e-mail user agents include:

- Eudora

- Pronto

- Pegasus Mail

- Microsoft Mail

All of these e-mail applications use a GUI and run in the Windows environment. Besides these e-mail applications, both Netscape Navigator and Microsoft Internet Explorer include mail user agent applications as well.

Regardless of the mail user agent used, common end-user configuration activities are setting up mail aliases, automatic forwarding, and filtering. Each of these is described in the following section.

### Mail Aliases

A mail alias enables you to set up an abbreviated name for frequently used or long and complicated e-mail addresses. Mail aliases are usually stored in a user-specific preference file (in the Solaris environment, the file is stored in `~/.mailrc`) and they are translated by the mail user agent before the mail is sent to the MTA. An alias usually takes the following form:

```
alias <name> <address1>, <address2> ...
```

An alias can be an abbreviation for one or more addresses. The mechanism used to set up an e-mail alias differs depending on the mail user agent used. Usually, it is located in the preferences or configuration menu option of the mail user agent. For example, in `mailtool`, an e-mail alias is set up using a menu in Edit ➤ Properties, while Microsoft's Exchange has it under Tools ➤ Address Book. The MTA also can set up a site wide alias for general use, described in *Setting Up the Mail Transfer Agent* on page 207.

### Mail Forwarding

A mail user agent application can be configured to automatically forward received mail to another user agent (this practice can pose a security risk within the intranet if messages are forwarded outside the intranet, and it should be discouraged). Since the mail user agent may not be running at all times, mail forwarding is configured by instructing the MTA to forward the mail.

Under Solaris, this is performed by setting up a ~/.forward file with the new destination address, which simply contains a new e-mail address.

In other operating environments, mail forwarding is accomplished by explicitly enabling this capability in the MTA's configuration file (described in *Setting Up the Mail Transfer Agent* on page 207).

### Mail Filtering and Auto Reply

Another common user mail agent function is to filter mail based on subject, contents, sender address, and so on. This helps you manage and prioritize large quantities of e-mail by automatically categorizing and filing e-mail messages in files and folders.

In cases where an immediate reply is required, you can set up automatic reply notification for all incoming messages, or specific incoming messages. An example is automatically replying to messages while you are away from your e-mail. If you are responsible for answering requests for technical support using e-mail, you could set up an automated e-mail response to acknowledge the receipt of a request for help.

For both mail filtering and auto reply functions, the ~/.forward file is used in the Solaris environment (in Windows, these capabilities are usually configured using the mail user agent, and the mechanism used differs depending on the mail user agent). You can specify a program to be executed by the MTA upon receipt of mail in this file. In the ~/.forward file shown in the following example, a program is used to automatically reply to messages.

```
\user-name, "|/usr/bin/vacation user-name"
```

As a result, any incoming e-mail message sent to *user-name* invokes the vacation program, which automatically sends a standard reply (the backslash (\) character that appears before *user-name* inhibits further aliasing).

In a similar fashion, you can use other programs to process incoming e-mail using the ~/.forward file. Consider the following example.

```
"|IFS=' ' && exec /usr/local/bin/procmail -f- || exit 75 #user-name"
```

The procmail[1] command filters incoming e-mail messages and stores them to mail folders based on message attributes such as subject header, sender address, and keywords that appear in the message contents. For example, you can configure procmail to store messages from your boss to a single mail folder. The ~/.procmailrc file is used to configure procmail, as shown below.

```
MAILDIR=$HOME/Mail
LOGFILE=$MAILDIR/inmail.log

:0:
* ^TOmkt-talk
in.mkt-talk
```

This file instructs procmail to deposit any incoming messages sent from the mkt-talk e-mail address into the folder in.mkt-talk. The entries in the ~/.procmailrc file are described in Table 13-1.

**Table 13-1** procmail **Mail Filtering Commands**

| Command | Description |
| --- | --- |
| :0 | Begin a recipe |
| : | Use a lock file |
| * | Begin a condition |
| ^TO | Match "To:", "Cc:" or other synonyms for "To" at the beginning of a line, followed by any or no characters. |

---

1. For details on how to further configure procmail, visit http://www.jazzie.com/ii/internet/procmail/. Source code and binaries are available at this web site.

# Setting Up the Mail Transfer Agent

We'll describe how to set up the MTA on a Solaris server so that mail user agent software running on any type of operating environment (such as Windows, Solaris, and others) can send and retrieve e-mail. For simplicity's sake, we'll refer to the MTA as the mail server in this procedure.

In a typical Solaris environment, the mail server is an NFS server that shares the *mail spool* area, or the directory used to store the user's incoming e-mail in files called or mailboxes. Mail user agents can access the mailboxes using NFS, or they can access them using a special e-mail protocol such as the Post Office Protocol (POP) or the Interactive Mail Access Protocol (IMAP), described in *Setting Up POP3 and IMAP4 Services* on page 208.

Setting up the mail server also involves creating a mail spool area, where incoming e-mail messages are stored. You should select a server system with sufficient disk space for each user mailbox in the /var/mail directory (usually, 2 Mbytes per user is sufficient).

## *Mail Server Procedures*

1. **Log into the mail server as root.**

2. **Set the directory permissions of the /var/mail directory to read / write with the sticky bit enabled.**
   Setting the sticky bit permits only the owner of the mailbox or the administrator to rename or delete the file, while it enables access for all desktop systems running mail user agents.

```
# chmod 1777 /var/mail
```

3. **Edit the /etc/dfs/dfstab file and add the following entry.**

```
# share -F nfs -o rw /var/mail
```

4. **Share the /var/mail directory to the desktops using NFS.**

```
# shareall
```

**5.** Start the NFS server processes.

```
# /etc/init.d/nfs.server stop
# /etc/init.d/nfs.server start
```

### Desktop Procedures for NFS-Based Mail Access

Use the following steps to configure NFS access to the mail server for each Solaris desktop. If the desktop uses POP or IMAP4 to access mail, skip these steps.

**1.** Log into the Solaris desktop as root.

**2.** Verify that the /var/mail directory is accessible.

```
# /usr/sbin/dfshares mail-server
```

**3.** Edit the /etc/vfstab file and the following entry.

```
mail-server:/var/mail - /var/mail nfs - yes -
```

**4.** Mount the mail server.

```
# mount /var/mail
```

## Setting Up POP3 and IMAP4 Services

POP3 and IMAP4[2] provide a method other than using NFS to transfer mail to the mail user agent. POP3 and IMAP4 are also well suited for environments where users access mail over slow connections, such as PPP-based links.

You should configure the mail server with both POP3 and IMAP4 support, since many mail user agent applications (especially for those available for Windows) often use these protocols to access mail. The IMAP4 server is provided with the Solstice Internet Mail[3] Server software, and the POP3 server is available in the Solstice PC-NFS software.

2. For more information, visit http://www.imc.org/imap4/.
3. For more information,
   visit http://www.sun.com/sunsoft/solstice/int_mail.html. A time-restricted evaluation copy is freely available.

### Setting Up IMAP4 Services

1.  **Log into the Solaris mail server as root.**

2.  **Add the IMAP4 package.**
    Consult the Solstice documentation for the location of the `SUNWimap` package.

```
# pkgadd -d `pwd` SUNWimap
```

Answer 'yes' to any questions

3.  **Add an entry for the IMAP service to the** `/etc/services` **file.**

```
imap 143/tcp imap #Interactive Mail Access Port
```

4.  **Add an entry for the IMAP daemon to the** `/etc/inetd.conf` **file.**

```
map stream tcp nowait root /usr/sbin/imapd imapd
```

The mail server is now capable of providing access to incoming mail stored in mailboxes using the NFS and IMAP4 protocols. An added benefit is heterogeneity—the mail server is a capable of providing services to mail user agents running on multiple platforms, including Windows.

The procedure to add POP3 services is similar to the steps described in this section—consult the Solstice PC-NFS documentation for more information.

## Setting Up E-mail Aliases

As we mentioned earlier, e-mail aliases and e-mail forwarding can also be set up on the MTA. It's easier to administer a large alias, such as a mail list, if it is set up on the server. An added benefit to storing an alias on the server is that any e-mail user can use the alias, unlike an alias stored in the user's `~/.mailrc` file, for example. Also, you can set up a forwarding address for obsolete accounts left behind by transferred users.

The Solaris environment provides a GUI named Database Manager to configure e-mail aliases and forwarding addresses stored in the `/etc/mail/aliases` file. An example is shown in Figure 13-1. This is the primary MTA configuration file we'll use in the next example.

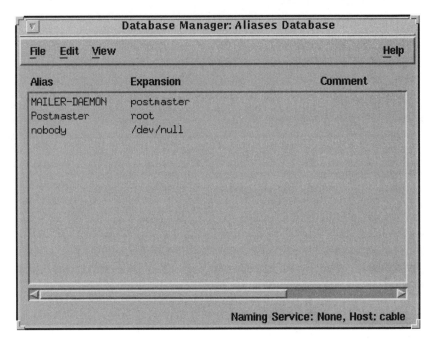

**Figure 13-1** Database Manager

An e-mail alias uses a number of formats. The following example uses the simplest form.

```
mktng: joe.smith@east, anne.baker@central, ...
```

E-mail sent to mktng@*mail-server* (the server where the alias is stored) is sent to the recipient joe.smith@east and anne.baker@central.

The next example uses a file to store recipient addresses.

```
finance: :include: /usr/local/finance-users.txt
```

All e-mail sent to finance@*mail-server* is sent to the recipients listed in the finance-users.txt file. Each e-mail address in this file should appear on a single line, as shown below.

```
joe.smith@east
anne.baker@central
...
```

In this example, e-mail is sent to a program.

```
eng:  "|program-name"
```

The contents (including e-mail headers) of mail sent to eng@*mail-server* is input to the executable *program-name*.

To add entries to the /etc/mail/aliases file, you should use Database Manager. Database Manager updates the MTA, and it also updates the NIS or NIS+ aliases map (the newaliases(1M) command is also used to update the MTA).

When adding e-mail aliases to the MTA, you should consider using e-mail addresses in canonical form, as shown below.

```
FirstName.LastName@Site.Region.Company.COM.
```

E-mail addresses in canonical format are easier to use and remember, and promote standardization across the organization.

### *Verifying E-mail Addresses*

You can verify e-mail addresses and aliases set up on the MTA by sending test e-mail messages, or by using the `mconnect` command, as shown in Example 13-2.

**Example 13-2** Verifying E-mail Addresses Using `mconnect`

```
❶ mconnect mail-server
  connecting to host mail-server (<...ipaddress...>), port 25
  connection open
  220 mail-server Sendmail <...version..> ready at <...time...>
❷ expn mkt-talk
  250-Jim <jim>
❸ 250-Bob <bob>
  250-Jerry <jerry>
❹ quit
```

The commands used in Example 13-2 are described below.

❶  The `mconnect` command opens up a connection to *mail-server* using the SMTP port. Alternately, you can use the `telnet` *mail-server* `25` command to open the connection.

❷  The `expn` command expands the alias `mkt-talk`.

❸  The recipients in the alias are displayed.

❹  The connection is terminated.

## Summary

In this chapter, we have described how to set up e-mail services in the intranet. SMTP-based e-mail is ideal for the intranet—it is an open, proven technology that enables messaging across many different operating environments. The disadvantage is that it lacks many features found in a proprietary, LAN-based e-mail solution. This is a limitation you should be aware of, because many intranet users may demand functionality that is not available in an SMTP-based e-mail service, such as the ability to cancel a message after it is sent. To address this need, there are middle-ware products available that are gateways between proprietary LAN-based e-mail and SMTP.

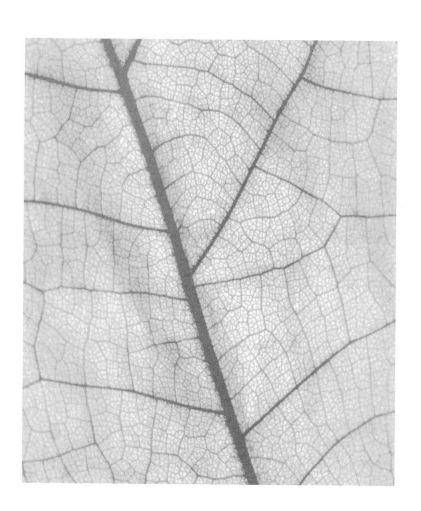

# CHAPTER 14

# MIME

In this chapter, we'll look at the Multipurpose Internet Mail Extension or MIME. MIME enables communication in an intranet using rich information types, such as video, audio, graphics, and so on. It accomplishes this by extending existing data types such as ASCII and technologies such as the Simple Mail Transfer Protocol (SMTP). We'll cover how MIME works, and how to configure e-mail and web services to fully utilize MIME capabilities.

## What is MIME?

MIME arose from the need to improve the quality of communication using e-mail in the Internet. Originally, e-mail was limited to the exchange of messages in simple ASCII text format. Though this is a tremendous advantage that allows interoperation and communication across a broad spectrum of operating environments and platforms, it can be limiting, especially since many users can now easily create and view multi-media content on their desktops. Rather than develop a new standard to handle the exchange of non-ASCII data types, the Internet governing body wisely chose to extending existing standards to accommodate this need, and created MIME[1]. The MIME standard supports the exchange of multi-part textual and non-textual messages without the loss of information.

### MIME Uses

MIME is attractive to users because it enables them to send and receive e-mail attachments containing pictures, sounds, and other non-ASCII file formats. Besides e-mail, MIME is also used in other applications where support for rich data types is useful, such as news readers and web browsers. In fact, MIME's importance has increased significantly with the popularity of the Web, since document types are specified using MIME for proper display in the web browser.

## The MIME Header

To indicate that a document supports MIME for proper use in e-mail, news reading, and Web browsing applications, information is added to the file header. The MIME header specifies the MIME version number for compatibility purposes, and information about the format of the document contents. At the very least, a MIME-compliant document must contain the following fields:

- A version field indicating compatibility, such as
  `MIME-Version: 1.0`

- A content field for each attachment, such as
  `Content-Type: type/subtype`

Following are the major data types supported by MIME:

- `application`
- `audio`
- `image`
- `message`
- `multipart`
- `text`
- `video`

---

1.  MIME has evolved as an Internet standard, and it has been accepted by the IETF. For more information, see http://www.internic.net/rfc/rfc1521.txt/ and http://www.internic.net/rfc/rfc1522.txt/.

To indicate a specific data type that is unique to an application, a MIME subtype is used. The subtype is a text string that indicates the type-specific data format, as shown in Example 14-1.

**Example 14-1** MIME Subtypes

```
Content-Type: image/gif
Content-Type: audio/x-pn-realaudio
Content-Type: video/mpeg
```

For a complete list of commonly used MIME types, please see Appendix A, MIME Types.

## Using MIME in E-mail

Let's look at how MIME headers are used in e-mail. As we discussed earlier, the key to supporting MIME in e-mail is to include the appropriate MIME type information in the header of the e-mail message. The MIME header is distinct from the standard e-mail headers used by the mail delivery system (see *Setting Up E-mail Services* on page 201). The MIME header information is followed by the MIME contents, commonly known as email attachments. The MIME header is processed by the mail reader to identify the type of attachment.

If a mail message contains a single attachment, the mail header also contains the MIME header. The MIME version number is specified in the first line of the MIME header for compatibility purposes, as shown in Example 14-2.

**Example 14-2** MIME Header, Single Attachment

```
Mime-Version: 1.0
....
Content-Type: TEXT/PLAIN; charset="US-ASCII"
Content-Length: 16287
```

If the e-mail message contains multiple attachments, each attachment is preceded by the `Content-Type` and `Content-Length` header fields (in addition to other MIME fields) as shown in Example 14-3.

**Example 14-3** MIME Header, Multiple Attachments

```
...
Content-Type: application/octet-stream; conversions="7bit"
Content-Description: instructions
Content-MD5: Yyf2DTcr1gG/Zt/Xlvj0Qw==
```

If it is capable of doing so, the mail reader can display the MIME data type on-screen. If it doesn't support this feature, the mail reader can start an external viewer application at the user's request and display the MIME contents.

### Mapping MIME Types to Viewer Applications

The mail reader must have some way of mapping a MIME data type to an external viewer application. This is done using a local file, where additional MIME type-to-application mappings can be easily configured. A typical file uses the format shown in Example 14-4.

**Example 14-4** MIME Type-to-Application Mappings File

```
audio/x-pn-realaudio; raplayer %s
audio/*; audiotool %s
image/*; imagetool %s
video/mpeg; mpeg_play %s
application/postscript; imagetool %s
application/pdf; acroread %s
```

The first field separated by a semi-colon indicates the MIME data type/sub-type. The second field indicates the external application that can read the data type. Notice that the MIME type-to-application mapping can be a many-to-one relationship, as indicated by the * character. If an external application is capable of handling most formats of a given MIME type, you don't need to specify a sub-type.

In Solaris, the MIME type-to-application mappings file is stored on a per-user base in $HOME/.mailcap. The mailcap file can also be used to specify mappings on a per site, system, or application basis.

In Windows, this information is stored in the HKEY_CLASSES_ROOT system registry using the following path:

---

MIME\Database\Content Type

---

MIME is also used in (NNTP) news, and the news reader handles MIME content in a similar fashion to an e-mail reader.

## Using MIME in the Web

As we mentioned earlier, MIME is not only used in e-mail and news, but it is also used by web servers and browsers. Since the web is a medium that heavily uses multiple content types, MIME plays an important role in ensuring that web browsers can work with different types of documents.

Most web pages use the following MIME type:

---

"text/html". Content-Type: text/html

---

### Viewing MIME Types In-Line

This MIME header is sent by the HTTP server to the web browser. Almost all web browsers can display HTML documents in-line, without the need for an external viewer application. Other types of documents that are also supported for in-line viewing include graphic documents. Both image/gif and image/tiff are two common MIME types that are viewed in-line in a web browser, for example.

### Viewing MIME Types Using Plug-Ins

A plug-in enables a web browser to view a MIME document in-line that would normally require an external application viewer. For example, an audio plug-in allows the in-line playback of a MIME document that uses the audio/basic content type. Without the plug-in, the web browser must call an external application to play back the audio file. If the web browser is not capable of viewing a MIME document in-line, it can use a MIME type-to-application mapping file, just like a mail reader or news reader. Here's an example:

```
application/postscript; imagetool %s
application/pdf; acroread %s
```

## MIME and HTTP

Unlike e-mail documents, which are delivered using a store and forward model, web documents are retrieved on an on-demand basis. The MIME content-type is determined on a per-document basis during the transaction between the web browser and the HTTP server. When the web browser requests a document from the HTTP server, the server first sends header information before transmitting the document, as shown in Example 14-5.

**Example 14-5** HTTP Header

```
HTTP/1.0 200 Document follows
MIME-Version: 1.0
Server: xxxx http server
Date: Monday, 30-Sep-96 01:40:04 GMT
Content-Type: text/html
Content-Length: 837
Last-Modified: Sunday, 23-Oct-95 20:31:16 GMT
```

Using this information, the web browser displays the document in-line or with the application viewer specified in the MIME type-to-application mapping file. You can easily add support for additional MIME types using built-in web browser controls. For example, the Netscape Navigator General Preferences window is shown in Figure 14-1.

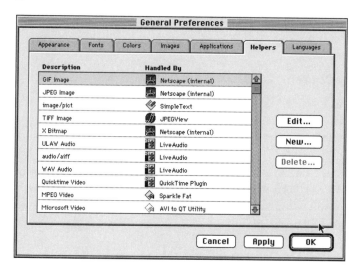

**Figure 14-1** Netscape Navigator 3.0 General Preferences Window

The Microsoft Internet Explorer Options window is shown in Figure 14-2.

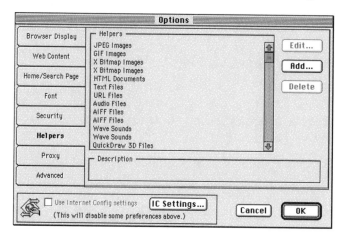

**Figure 14-2** Microsoft Internet Explorer 3.0 Options Window

## Identifying MIME Content-Types

Earlier, we described how the MIME content-type is determined on a per-document basis during a web transaction, and this information is enclosed in a MIME header. A question you might have is how does the HTTP server identify the content-type to begin with? Or, in an e-mail setting, how does the mail user agent identify the content-type for an attachment? The answer lies in understanding how content-types are dealt with in the native operating environment.

### *Identifying Content Types in E-mail – Solaris*

To understand how MIME content-types are identified in e-mail, let's use Solaris as an example. Solaris users can manage files using an OpenWindows-based application, File Manager. File and directories are presented in a graphical user interface, and the user can easily manipulate them. For example, by double-clicking on a file, the file is opened using the appropriate application viewer. File Manager performs this operation based on information stored in the `binder(1)`. The `binder` application defines viewers based on file extensions and the first few characters (4 bytes) of the file.

For example, the first characters that appear in a Postscript file are `!%`. The `binder` uses these characters to identify the content-type, much in the same way that the `file` command determines the file type. The `binder` can maintain this information on a per-user, system, and network basis. The `binder` also contains information about default icon files.

When the user includes an attachment in an e-mail message, the `binder` is consulted to create the MIME header for the attachment.

### *Identifying Content Types in E-mail – Windows*

In Windows, this information is stored in the system registry. Specifically, it resides in the Object Linking and Embedding (OLE) configuration portion of the `HKEY_CLASSES_ROOT` registry section. It can also be maintained on a per-user basis if user profiles are enabled.

The `MIME\Database\Content Type` section of the `HKEY_CLASSES_ROOT` registry contains the mapping information from the MIME type to the extension used by the document (for example, `.ps`, `.au`, and so on). It also contains the `CLASS ID` information for OLE. The reverse mapping information from extension to MIME type is also stored in the same tree.

## Identifying Content Types for Web Servers

An HTTP server identifies MIME content-types using internal configuration files. Example 14-6 shows the `mime.types` configuration file used by the Netscape HTTP server.

**Example 14-6** Netscape FastTrack Server `mime.types` File

```
type=application/octet-stream   exts=bin,exe
type=application/pdf            exts=pdf
type=application/postscript     exts=ai,eps,ps
type=application/rtf            exts=rtf
type=application/x-mif          exts=mif
type=application/x-csh          exts=csh
type=application/x-dvi          exts=dvi
type=application/x-sh           exts=sh
type=application/x-tcl          exts=tcl
```

Using this file, the Netscape server determines MIME content-type to file extension mappings, and creates the MIME header. For example, if a file ending in `.ps` is requested, the server uses the `mime.types` configuration file to construct the MIME header that specifies `application/postscript` as the content-type.

## Identifying Content Types for Web Browsers

Besides the negotiation that occurs between the HTTP server and the web browser, there is also explicit mapping that occurs on the web browser, based on URLs. For example, the following URL contains an extension that is mapped to the `application/postscript` content type.

```
file://localhost/file.ps
```

The web browser can interpret the `.ps` extension and request the appropriate viewer, without requiring a MIME header from the HTTP server.

This mapping is stored in the mailcap file, it is configurable on a per-user basis, and it is stored in `$HOME/.mime.types` in Solaris. For the sake of simplicity, you should maintain a site-wide mailcap file and make it available using NFS to all users with e-mail and web browsing capabilities.

For example, the Solaris version of Netscape Navigator can be configured to read the MIME information from a global file. To view this configuration window, select Options ➤ General Preferences ➤ Helpers in Netscape Navigator.

The global mailcap file can also be specified in the user's home directory. The $HOME/.netscape/preferences file can be configured as shown in Example 14-7.

**Example 14-7** Netscape Navigator preferences **File - Solaris**

```
MIME_TYPES:            /usr/local/lib/netscape/mime.types
PERSONAL_MIME_TYPES:   ~/.mime.types
MAILCAP:               /usr/local/lib/netscape/mailcap
PERSONAL_MAILCAP:      ~/.mailcap
```

## Summary

MIME enables communication in an intranet using diverse information types. It is an important component used by web browsers, web servers, and mail user agents to help ensure that users can easily access multiple data types. By properly configuring the user environment with the right MIME mapping information, you can prevent frustrating errors that users sometimes encounter when they access a web page or receive an e-mail message with an unrecognized file type.

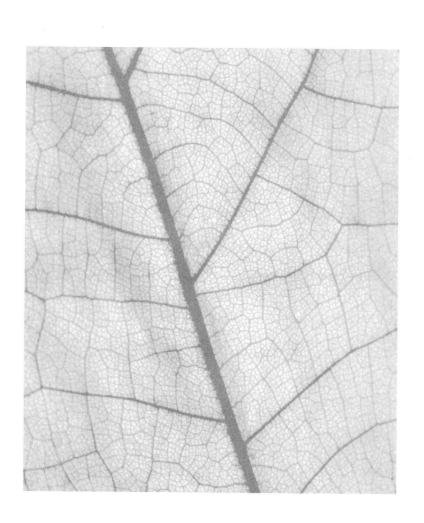

# CHAPTER 15

# Zero-Administration Clients

Computing in the corporation has evolved from a highly centralized architecture to the distributed computing environment we know today. The advent of low-cost microprocessors spawned the personal computing revolution, with users demanding local computing power on their desktops. Today's corporate desktop is a typically a PC or a workstation. The typical desktop has local disk storage, is attached to the network, and runs an operating system that is stored on the local disk. Though this configuration may be ideal for the user, it introduces formidable administration problems to the intranet administrator, such as installing and maintaining the operating system, backing up and restoring configuration files and user data, distributing application software, and so on. In past chapters, we've described techniques to manage these problems. In this chapter, we'll take a fresh look at the desktop computer by introducing *zero-administration clients*, systems that do not require local administration.

## The Desktop Computing Problem

As computing resources have become decentralized, so too has the control and administration of these resources. Many intranet administrators are faced with the ongoing challenge of administering distributed desktop clients while maintaining network resources and performance. Desktop administration tasks such as continually updating the OS, installing OS patches, installing software and dealing with incompatibilities is consuming an inordinate amount of the intranet administrator's time—up to 70%! This does not include other tasks, such as backing up and recovering data, and reinstalling the OS for each and every intranet desktop. Though an intranet lowers the cost of ownership in a distributed computing environment, intranet administrators are constantly looking for new techniques that will enable them to manage more clients per server, and replicate system support for a larger number of users.

This problem has not escaped the attention of the CIO, either. CIOs are painfully aware of the high cost of owning a desktop, and they are seeking ways to reduce or eliminate these costs. Many long for the days of mainframe and terminal-based computing, where all the data safely resided in a centralized location. With large, centralized computers, it was easy to maintain and update the software services provided to users. However, CIOs also recognize that users want local computing power and the benefits it brings, such as graphical user interfaces and powerful software applications. The ideal computing environment would incorporate the best features of each computing model, without any of the drawbacks.

Attempts to centralize system administration using a new computing model have had mixed results. For example, while diskless clients and X-terminals appeared attractive because they centralized administration on the server, the performance trade-offs and network loads they imposed were unacceptable to most users and administrators. The ideal solution would combine the benefits of centralized system administration while retaining the performance of distributed computing.

## Solstice AutoClient

Enter the world of Solstice AutoClient[1]. This product is based on the premise that the Solaris OS installed on the desktop is of very little interest to the average intranet user. Most users only care about the applications they run on a day-to-day basis to get their work done. If this is the case, why not remove the OS completely? Of course, the desktop can't function without the OS, but does the OS really need to permanently reside on the desktop? What if the desktop could load the OS from the network on an on-demand basis? You might say that this is just another example of a diskless client, but there is a critical difference. An AutoClient uses caching technology to overcome the server load and network bandwidth problems that plagued diskless clients.

---

1.   For more information, visit http://www.sun.com/sunsoft/solstice/em-products/system/autoclient-wp.html/.

AutoClients are an ideal choice for an intranet. AutoClients are typical desktop workstations, and they require only a small, under 200 Mbyte local disk. They deliver the same local computing power of a standard workstation without the administrative overhead of maintaining local data.

Data such as individual user files, software, and the OS all reside on the server. When the workstation accesses this data, it is copied to the local disk. All subsequent access to the same data occurs from the local disk after a quick check to ensure its integrity with the original version stored on the server. The OS software distribution and other software resides on the server, and only the components that are used by the desktop are copied to the local disk. If the local disk is full, the least-recently used components are deleted to make room for the newly-requested components. All this is done automatically using CacheFS, the cache file system[2].

If the local disk fails, the AutoClient is easily repaired by replacing the disk and rebooting from the network. If the processor or another motherboard component fails, the AutoClient is easily replaced by swapping in a new base unit, updating a single entry in a network database, and rebooting.

AutoClient systems can be installed using the 'disconnectable' feature. If the network or server is temporarily unavailable, the AutoClient system can continue to function as a non-networked, standalone system, queuing up its transactions until the network or server becomes available.

### AutoClient Installation

Installing an AutoClient system is trivial. Using the Host Manager GUI, you add a new host using the AutoClient system type, and provide the ethernet and IP address of the machine to be installed. An example is shown Figure 15-1.

---

2.   For more information, visit http://www.sun.com/smcc/solaris-migration/tools/docs/courses/sysadminHTML/cachefs.html/.

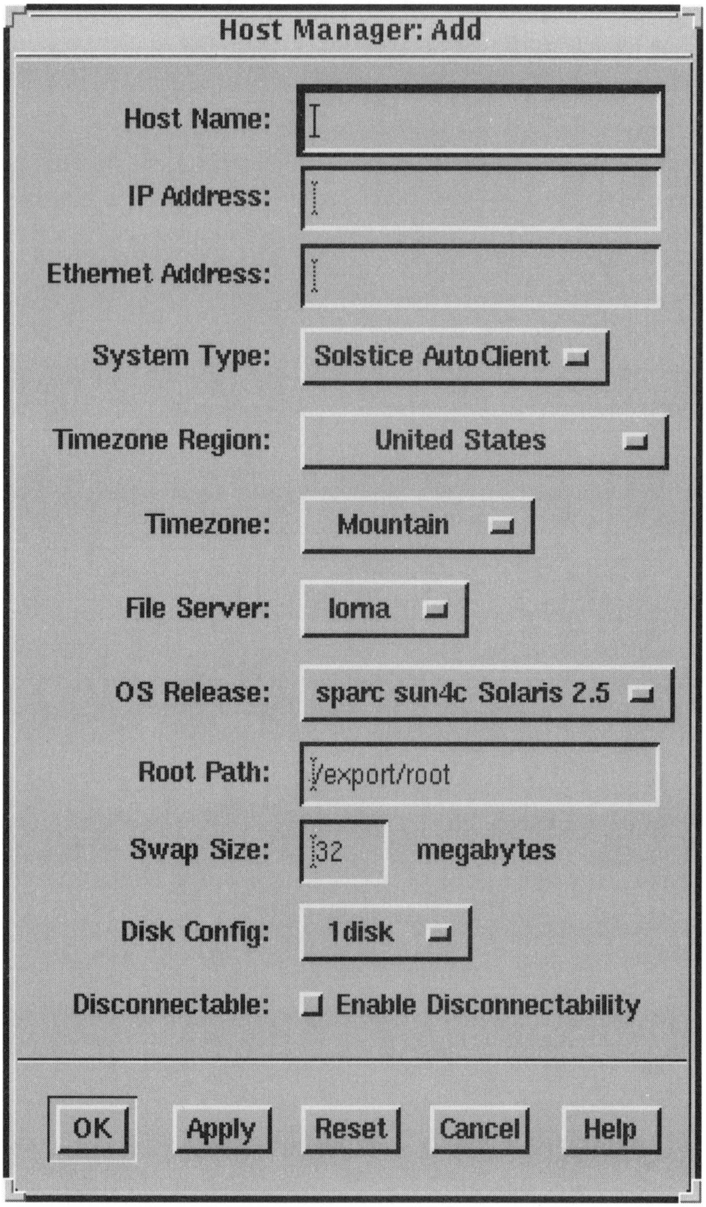

**Host Manager: Add**

Host Name:

IP Address:

Ethernet Address:

System Type:    Solstice AutoClient

Timezone Region:    United States

Timezone:    Mountain

File Server:    lorna

OS Release:    sparc sun4c Solaris 2.5

Root Path:    /export/root

Swap Size:    32    megabytes

Disk Config:    1disk

Disconnectable:    Enable Disconnectability

OK    Apply    Reset    Cancel    Help

**Figure 15-1** AutoClient Installation Using Host Manager

Then, boot the desktop over the network by typing `boot net` at the OpenBoot `ok` prompt. Before it is ready for use, the client automatically performs these activities:

- Searches the local subnet for its server

- Retrieves the files needed to bootstrap itself

- Creates a cache on the local disk using CacheFS

- Mounts the Solaris OS distribution and associated files from the specified server

- Starts the operating system, and presents a login service

### *AutoClient Updates*

You can also update files on the server and push them to all the AutoClients. Alternatively, the AutoClients can elect to receive updates at a specified time. This mechanism enables you to control the user's desktop operating environment in a centralized manner, and the desktop user is freed from having to administer or troubleshoot their system.

### *AutoClient Limitations*

AutoClients aren't for everyone. For example, AutoClients that are the same platform group (for example, Sun4c) share parts of the operating system from a common directory on a read-only basis. This can be a problem for "power" users who commonly add software packages that require write access to this directory. For this reason, the AutoClient system type may not be suitable for users who need more control over their operating environment. These users are better served with a standalone system. Also, AutoClients based on the Intel x86 platform need a boot floppy to automatically boot without any user intervention, such as after a power failure.

Solstice AutoClient is the first in a wave of centralized host administration solutions aimed at lowering the cost of owning a desktop. Solstice AutoClient runs in the Solaris 2.5 operating environment or greater, and supports clients based on the SPARC and Intel x86 platforms.

## The Cost of Owning a Desktop PC

Now, let's consider the case of a desktop PC running Windows. To survive in the intranet, Windows desktop users need to know much more than the location of the on/off switch on their PCs. For example, here are some of the tasks that must be performed to restore the system in the event of a disk crash:

- Boot from floppy

- Use the `fdisk` command to reformat the local disk

- Create a boot device by installing the correct network or CD-ROM drivers for the desktop hardware configuration

- Mount the network file system or CD-ROM as a drive and run `setup`

- Know which software components are required, select them, and wait an hour to install the OS and reboot the machine

If a mistake is made almost anywhere in the process, almost all these steps must be repeated. But there's more! After the OS is installed, any OS patches such as service packs must also be installed. Finally, any application software such as MS Office, VC++, and so on is installed. When the OS changes, the whole process is repeated, with users hoping that their software applications don't break in the new operating environment.

This is an example of the true cost of owning a desktop PC. The initial cost of the hardware and software is usually much less than the cost of the administrator's time spent maintaining the desktop.

## Enter the JavaStation

The advent of the Web, Java, and rising desktop PC ownership costs have introduced a new twist in the centralized administration model. Many vendors are re-evaluating desktop computing, and companies such as Sun are re-inventing the concept of the desktop computer. Sun wants you to view a desktop computer like another item commonly found on the desktop—the telephone.

When you use a telephone, you are using a communications appliance. You aren't concerned about the myriad of technical issues being resolved in the background. For example, the switching that is done at the central office to connect you to the person you wish to speak to happens transparently. You don't need to know about or even care that your conversation is digitized into thousands of small containers called packets and that these packets are routed across vast telecommunications networks.

When the telephone breaks, you plug in a new one, with no change in service.

What if you could treat a desktop computer in just this way? The machine that sits on a user's desk is simply a computing appliance. From the user's point of view, the technical wizardry that makes it work is hidden, yet all the services the user is accustomed to are still available. For the moment, assume that the desktop machine is an appliance, like a telephone. Now, from an intranet administrator's point of view, that means you need not focus your efforts on managing that appliance, but on the services required by that appliance. All the maintenance that is performed on the desktop computer today can be moved to the server back end.

The JavaStation is designed to be a zero administration desktop appliance, just like a telephone. The JavaStation Tower contains no disks, floppies, or tape drives, and only requires a network connection. Available for a very low cost, it has a monitor, a keyboard, and a small footprint base unit that has 8 Mbytes of memory and a SPARC processor, as shown in Figure 15-2.

**Figure 15-2** The JavaStation Tower

### *JavaStation Benefits*

The JavaStation desktop offers many compelling advantages to intranet administrators and users:

- All OS updates are performed on the server.
  - New versions can be released at any time
  - No components are stored on the client
- All software updates are performed by the provider.
  - New versions can be released at any time
  - Users simply click and use the latest version of the software
  - No application is stored on the client
- Printing services are provided using existing network printers.
  - No configuration is necessary because the NIS printer configuration is used

- Local computing power is provided.

  — Users are limited only by the local processor speed and network bandwidth

  — JavaStations with local disks used for caching purposes reduce network bandwidth and are limited by processor speed only.

JavaStations can be added incrementally, without having to discard existing hardware or software investments. For example, existing desktop computers such as Windows PCs and Solaris workstations can share the web services along with JavaStations within the intranet. New desktop computer investments can be solely JavaStations.

### The HotJava Views User Environment

The default user environment for the JavaStation is HotJava™ Views™ 1.0. It runs in the JavaOS™ operating environment used by the JavaStation, and it provides e-mail, calendaring, name directory access, and web browsing capabilities in an intuitive and easy-to-use environment. An example is shown in Figure 15-3.

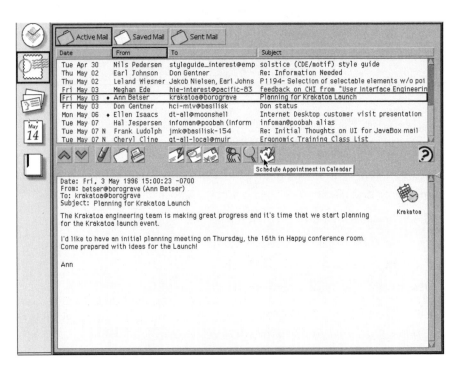

**Figure 15-3** HotJava Views – MailView

Here are just a few of the benefits this environment brings to the intranet:

- Zero administration

  All of the software is installed and configured on the back-end server, and no client-side administration is necessary. Using the included administration tools, you can define user profiles and establish what software is available to each user at login time.

- Minimal software distribution costs

  The software is upgraded on the server, and the clients "pull" the software only when it is needed. This eliminates the need to maintain software on each client, and promotes a centralized administration model.

- Easy desktop computer replacement

  If the JavaStation hardware fails, there is no need to restore the operating system or any configuration data, since it is stored on the server. You simply plug in a new unit, and the user resumes the work session, since the state of the user environment is continually saved.

The HotJava Views user environment can also be easily extended with custom or third-party Java solutions.

## Setting Up the JavaStation Server

This section provides an overview of the tasks required to set up JavaStation services using a Solaris server. Perform this procedure only if you wish to add JavaStation services to a pre-existing Solaris server. If you are using the Netra-J[3] server, note that it is pre-configured to support JavaStation clients, and no additional software installation or configuration is necessary.

### Task Prerequisites

- Verify that the Solaris OS release running on the server is version 2.5 or greater.

- Verify that the Dynamic Host Configuration Protocol (DHCP) and Federated Naming System (FNS) software packages are installed.

- Obtain the JavaStation services software package

- If the server uses a BOOTP server that was not installed from the `SUNWjdse` package, and that server is started by an `init` script at boot time, disable that script since it will interfere with the DHCP services.

---

3.  For more information, visit http://www.sun.com/products-n-solutions/hw/servers/netra.html/netra_j/index.html/.

*Task Overview*

- Install the JavaStation services software package
- Configure the server using the JavaStation Manager GUI
- Install the JavaStation using the JavaStation Manager GUI
- Boot the JavaStation

## Installing the JavaStation Server Software

1. **Log into the server as root.**

2. **Verify that the server is running Solaris 2.5 or greater.**
   An example is shown below.

```
# uname -a
SunOS server-name 5.5.1 Generic sun4m sparc SUNW,SPARCstation-10
```

3. **Verify that the DHCP and FNS software is installed.**

```
# pkginfo SUNWdhcsr SUNWdhscu SUNWfns
```

The SUNWfns package is part of the standard Solaris 2.5 or 2.5.1 OS distribution. The SUNWdhcsr and SUNWdhcsu packages are available in Solaris 2.5.1 ISS (Internet Server Supplement) OS distribution. If necessary, obtain and install this software.

4. **Install the JavaStation services software package.**
   You can obtain the Solaris SUNWjdse software package in tar format from your Sun sales channels. To unpack and install the software, use the commands shown below.

```
# tar xvf SUNWjdse.tar
# pkgadd -d `pwd` SUNWjdse
```

## Configuring the JavaStation Server

1. **Launch the OpenWindows environment or a similar X-Windows environment if you have not already done so.**

```
# /usr/openwin/bin/openwin
```

**2.   Start the JavaStation Manager GUI.**

```
# /opt/SUNWjdse/bin/jdhostmgr
```

The JavaStation Manager GUI is displayed.

```
╔══════════════════════════════════════════════════╗
║          JavaStation Manager: Set Defaults          ║
╠══════════════════════════════════════════════════╣
║                                                    ║
║      DNS Domain Name: [I                        ]  ║
║                                                    ║
║  DNS Server IP Address: [                       ]  ║
║                                                    ║
║         Subnet Mask: [                          ]  ║
║                                                    ║
║      Router IP Address: [                       ]  ║
║                                                    ║
║                                                    ║
║        [OK] [Apply] [Reset] [Cancel] [Help]        ║
╚══════════════════════════════════════════════════╝
```

**3.   Type in the defaults for the JavaStation environment.**
You need to set the defaults for the JavaStation environment for the
following network parameters:

- **DNS domain name**

    Example: Sales.MyCompany.COM

    To obtain the domain name, use the `domainname` command.

- **DNS server's IP address**

    Example: 129.132.221.1

    To obtain the DNS server's IP address, use the `nslookup` command.

- **Subnet Mask**

    Example: 255.255.255.0

    To obtain the subnet mask, use the `ifconfig -a` command.

- **Router IP Address**

    Example: 129.132.221.254

To obtain the router IP address, use the `netstat -nr` and look for your subnet address.

**4.** **Click OK.**
After applying changes, the message `Defaults Update Pending` is displayed in the lower right corner of the window.

**5.** **Select Edit ➤ Add to add JavaStation clients.**
The Add window is displayed.

```
┌─────────────────────────────────────────────────────┐
│            JavaStation Manager: Add                  │
│                                                      │
│      Host Name:  [I                              ]   │
│                                                      │
│     IP Address:  [                               ]   │
│                                                      │
│ Ethernet Address: [                              ]   │
│                                                      │
│         OK  Apply  Reset  Cancel  Help               │
└─────────────────────────────────────────────────────┘
```

You must specify a name, an IP address, and a corresponding hexadecimal Ethernet address for each JavaStation client. To obtain the Ethernet address, consult the configuration sheet that was shipped with the system.

**6.** **Click Apply to add each client entry.**
The host list window is updated with each new entry, and a + symbol to the left of each entry indicates that the operation is pending.

```
 ┌────────────────────────────────────────────────────────┐
 │ ▽         JavaStation Manager                           │
 ├────────────────────────────────────────────────────────┤
 │  File   Edit   View   Help                              │
 │ ┌──────────────────────────────────────────────────────┤
 │ │   Host              IP Address         Ethernet Address │
 │ │ + arnold            128.146.101.104    08:00:20:0a:0b:0c │
 │ │   newken            128.146.101.105    08:00:20:7c:ba:99 │
 │ │                                                        │
 │ ├──────────────────────────────────────────────────────┤
 │ │ + add, - delete, | modify                             │
 │ │ Total Changes Pending: 1                              │
 └──────────────────────────────────────────────────────────┘
```

**7.** **Select File ➤ Save Changes to save and write the changes.**
The pending changes are committed, and the new clients are added.

**8.** **Reboot the JavaStation by cycling the power switch.**
The JavaStation automatically queries the network to obtains its name and IP address, locates the server, and loads the latest version of the JavaOS. After booting, a login window is displayed.

Complete this step, and you're done.

Because the JavaStation client uses NIS naming services, any existing NIS user name and password can be used to log into the system. After logging in, the HotJava Views environment is displayed. At this point, the entire intranet is accessible to the user, and any Java-based application can be used.

## JavaStation Deployment

As you can imagine, migrating from a traditional desktop computing environment to one based on Java and JavaStation is not a trivial endeavor. Fortunately, help is available, and you can find white papers, demos, product overviews, and other information at the Sun Java Computing web site[4]. Here are

---

4. For more information, visit http://www.sun.com/javacomputing/.

some recommendations culled from this web site to help you successfully transition to a centralized administration model using zero-administration JavaStation clients.

- Start by building an intranet infrastructure
- Deploy Java-based applications throughout the intranet, initially using Java-enabled web browsers
- Migrate e-mail to the intranet using the SMTP/IMAP4 protocols
- Develop Java competence in the IS organization through training
- Defer mass desktop OS upgrades. Instead, perform selective upgrades for specific applications or users
- Watch for new product announcements from developers of Java-based applications[5]
- Identify applications that are used to perform critical business functions; port these to Java, and introduce JavaStations to the users
- Use X-Windows server software on JavaStations to enable access to legacy applications that have not been ported to Java
- Ensure that new IS proposals for systems or application changes or upgrades also include Java-based options
- Start replacing traditional desktops with JavaStations after establishing a critical mass of Java-based applications

## Summary

In this chapter, we've examined alternatives to the traditional desktop computer. Solstice AutoClient is the first in a wave of high performance desktops that do not require local administration. Since data such as the operating system, software applications, and user files are never persistently stored on the local disk, a centralized administration model is possible. While Solstice AutoClient provides a Solaris end-user operating environment in a package that is easier and cheaper to administer, the JavaStation is a more radical alternative centered on the "write-once, distribute anywhere" Java computing model. JavaStations are easily replaceable, low cost, network computing appliances that free intranet administrators from the costly cycle of constant desktop computer maintenance. Problems such as upgrading the OS and application software, backing up and restoring user files, and troubleshooting software incompatibilities are eliminated, resulting in a significantly lower cost of ownership for the corporation.

5.   To see an example of a desktop productivity application written purely in Java, visit http://officeforjava.corel.com/.

# PART FOUR

## Building Web Services

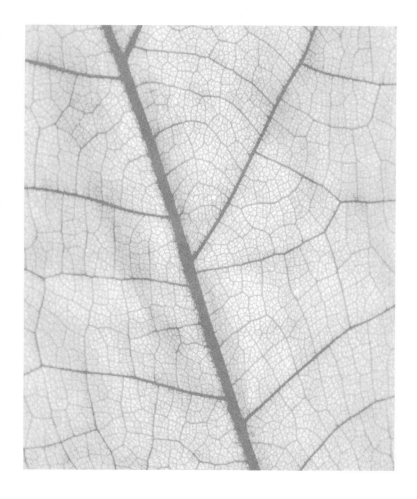

# CHAPTER 16

# Web Services

T his chapter is an overview of the web services your organization can use to communicate with itself. We'll examine the client/server model used for web services, and describe other useful web-based services based on protocols other than HTTP. Security is an important concern when dealing with sensitive information, so we'll describe encryption schemes that guarantee the safety of network transactions. Since it is likely that intranet users will convert existing documents to HTML format and publish them on the internal web, we'll also describe HTML conversion utilities. Finally, we'll present a method for administering web services in a centralized and consistent manner.

## The Web Client / Server Model

As you may have realized by now, the Web has a client/server architecture. The simplest model has the client requesting a URL using the following format.

---

*protocol://server:port/path/page.extension*

---

This URL sends a request using a *protocol* such as HTTP to the *server*, on a specified *port* for a specific *page* using an *extension* in the *path*. The server then sends the client information about the requested page, such as the following:

- Mime-type

  See *MIME* on page 215.

- Expiration date

  This value specifies when the page contents must be obtained directly from the server before they can be displayed in the web browser.

- Last modified time

  This value indicates the last time the page contents were modified.

The server sends the page to the client and closes the connection. A key difference from other client/server architectures is the web client's ability to simultaneously communicate with many servers at the same time to display a page. This is an important feature that enables transparent document integration and scalability.

Using the web model for distributing information in an intranet, information is published once in a centralized manner in the location known as the web site. Users interested in the information retrieve it on-demand. The information is updated centrally on the web server, and there is no need to forward the updates to interested parties using e-mail and similar methods.

### Benefits

- Since information is stored in a centralized location, it is easier to keep it up-to-date

- Users can retrieve the information when they need it. The user, not the information publisher, decides when the information is required.

### Disadvantages

- Alerts

  Information publishers need to advertise new web sites or updates to an existing web site. Information publishers can't assume the people they want to reach are aware of the web site.

  Though there are ways to advertise a web site such as sending the URL using e-mail and requesting that people visit the web site, there is no guarantee that the information will reach the audience.

## Types of Web Services

Most web services are based on a user-centric, information on-demand client/server model. Unlike other intranet services such as e-mail, Web services enable users to retrieve only if they deem it useful, and they retrieve it at their convenience.

### The Hyper Text Transfer Protocol (HTTP)

HTTP is a protocol that transfers Hyper Text Markup Language (HTML) to the requesting system. An HTML-capable viewer application such as the Netscape Navigator Web browser renders the HTML and formats the information for display on the screen.

A file transfer service is also supported by HTTP. With a combination of the HTTP protocol and Multi Internet Media Exchange (MIME) types, you can implement sophisticated file transfer services (see *MIME* on page 215). MIME involves mapping file name extensions such as `.mov` and `.au` to an action on the client system.

When a file is transferred using HTTP that matches the MIME type specified on the requesting system, the file is opened using a specified action. An example action is launching an audio player application to play a file ending with `.au` extension. If no action is specified, the file requestor window is opened and the user can save the file (this is the default action).

### Secondary Web Services

- File Transfer Protocol (FTP)

  This protocol is primarily intended for transferring large files from one system to another. It is not a file sharing service, but it allows you to perform the following file management activities:

  - Browse directories
  - Transfer files
  - Remove files
  - Rename files

- Gopher

  Gopher is a precursor to HTTP and has largely been made obsolete by HTTP. This protocol got its start in the university environment. Similar to HTTP, it uses a Web model, and lists information in a manner similar to bulletin-board menu systems. Unlike HTTP, where text and images can be embedded with hypertext links, the gopher system allows only links.

  Since gopher does a good job of cataloging large amounts of information, gopher services are found in environments where this capability is useful, such as university, government BBS, and library environments.

  Gopher works like the early version of the CompuServe network, where users navigated to special interest areas by using the 'go' command. Instead of using this command, users access links to take them to areas containing different information.

- Network News Transfer Protocol (NNTP)

  This protocol is useful for broadcasting low-priority, public information. USENET is the Internet implementation of NNTP, and works like a world-wide bulletin board system. News servers retrieve news articles and store the files locally for news readers to view at their leisure. The servers also transfer files to other servers if need be.

  NNTP can be used in an intranet to distribute low priority information. You can set up a private hierarchy of newsgroups that contain subjects of interest to internal organizations only (these newsgroups are usually not redistributed outside the company firewall).

## Web Security

Security is different than access control. Access control uses simple methods that can be bypassed, while security uses encryption schemes to guarantee that a network transaction is not intercepted by unauthorized persons.

### Secure HTTP

The Netscape Commerce Server provides secure network transactions using Secure HTTP (SHTTP). Using SHTTP, the user is authenticated at login time. The server uses the login name and password for the duration of the session. The server creates a secure socket, and all further communication between the client and server uses the secure socket. This secure transaction layer is also known as the *secure socket layer* (SSL). Both the Netscape Navigator and Internet Explorer web browsers support this feature.

### Certificates

In this scheme, the user is authenticated by a third party authority. The user is granted a certificate that is only valid for the duration of the transaction between the client and server. After the transaction is completed, the certificate is destroyed.

### Subscriptions

Subscription-based security is commonly used for web sites that charge a fee to use their services, such as commercial newspaper and magazine web sites, such as the New York Times or Wall Street Journal.

The user is authenticated using information stored in a 'cookie' that is passed from the web browser to the server. After examining the cookie, the server grants the user access. Using the cookie, the user doesn't have to be authenticated each time he or she accesses the web site.

An example of a subscription-based service in an intranet is a web site that offers employee benefits information. Access to areas that contain sensitive information can be restricted to managers only using a subscription-based authentication mechanism.

Pages that access information stored in databases can be restricted in a similar manner. Sensitive information found in an intranet such as payroll, 401K, the stock purchase plan, and similar information can be protected using any of the security methods described in this section.

## HTML Conversion Tools

In this section, we won't describe how to write documents using HTML or the HTML syntax, but we will describe several utilities that convert existing documents into HTML.

Most people can quickly master HTML, and the plethora of easy-to-use HTML editors and HTML conversion utilities is opening up the world of web publishing to all sorts of users with little or no technical experience. The Web gives individuals within an intranet, as well the organization itself, the power to be information providers.

There are several word processing tools that produce HTML output in addition to PostScript, Rich Text Format (RTF), or printed documents. Most of the tools for converting documents from word processor formats to HTML are not complete. Since HTML is very limited in formatting and layout, you cannot expect the same look and feel in the converted document. Success rate varies with the type of document and its contents. Almost all the tools map paragraph styles in a document to a series of HTML directives that produce a similar looking web page.

- Adobe FrameMaker 5.x

  This desktop publishing application allows you to save FrameMaker documents to HTML using a conversion utility named HoTaMaLe (http://www.adobe.com/prodindex/framemaker/).

- Microsoft Word 7.0

  This word processing application can save word (or RTF) documents in HTML format. It can also act as a web browser and view a document into its viewing area. You can then edit the contents including images as you would with a regular Word document. The Microsoft Internet Assistant Web publishing software is available as a free add-on package, and it can be found at the Microsoft web site (http://www.microsoft.com/msword/internet/ia/).

- Netscape Navigator Gold

  Netscape offers this combined web browser/editor software (http://home.mcom.com/comprod/mirror/client_download.html/). You can browse a page, and then save the contents for editing.

None of these tools provide a complete solution, but they are a good way to start the process of generating HTML documents.

Applications that are specifically designed for creating and managing web documents are already showing up on the market. An excellent example is NetObjects Fusion (http://www.netobjects.com/). This web authoring/site management software comes with several pre-designed templates to enable you to quickly get started publishing web content. It also provides an excellent user interface for editing and adding information. You can edit and place audio, video, graphics, Java applets, and other components using the software, and then generate the HTML pages and view them in a web browser like Netscape Navigator.

All of the software we've described eliminates the need to code in HTML manually. These software utilities and applications do an excellent job of generating HTML, and they provide style templates and WYSIWYG editing and placement of web page elements such as tables, lists, and image alignments. Of course, individual components such as Java applets, audio and video clips, and images may need to be created separately.

## Web Service Administration

### Naming Web Servers

Using a name space, you can map a descriptive name to the IP address of a server in your intranet that provides a web service. For example, the following names can be used to describe web server functions in the DNS environment.

**Table 16-1** DNS Mappings – Web Services

| Web Service | DNS Server Name |
|-------------|-----------------|
| FTP | ftp.finance.xyz.com |
| GOPHER | gopher.legal.xyz.com |
| HTTP | www.marketing.xyz.com |

You can easily relocate web services in your Intranet using the name space by re-mapping server IP addresses (see *Setting Up Domain Name Services* on page 167).

### *Web Site Organization*

The information stored on an intranet web server tends to grow quickly, and it can become difficult to manage and update over time. Information that you lose track of can become outdated and essentially useless. An undesirable side-effect of outdated information is that users visiting the web site can quickly become frustrated and impatient if they have to wade through pages of meaningless information before they find what they need.

To avoid these problems, you should organize information so that it is easily manageable when you first set up the web server.

For example, information can be organized using the following parameters:

- Function
    - Engineering
    - Finance
    - Marketing
- Organization
- Geography
- And so on

You can choose any combination of these parameters, based on the needs of your organization. An example intranet home page is shown in Figure 16-1.

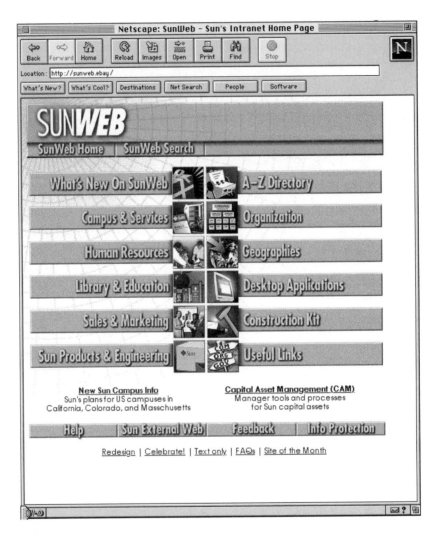

**Figure 16-1** SunWeb Home Page

### Web Site Consistency

Users can navigate through the web site more easily and find the information they seek more quickly if each page has common navigation controls. A common look and feel does not necessarily mean the use of graphic design in the pages. Instead, it means the consistent placement of information and controls on each page. For example, the footer on each page can contain a link that takes the user to a feedback page. The header on each page can contain navigational links to the top level of the web site information hierarchy, and so on.

To enable a common look and feel for all Intranet Web pages, you should provide a set of HTML templates to content providers, or the individuals who need to publish information in an intranet using web services. A typical template file contains company logo, company address, copyright information, and so on. Users simply copy the template from a central location to their home directories, and edit the file by adding their content.

Using HTML templates reduces the time it takes to author and publish information. Administrators don't have to become Web masters, or Web experts, themselves, either.

### The Centralized Web Administration Model

Surveys indicate that the proliferation of web services is mostly a grass roots, bottom-up effort for most organizations. This is largely due to the ease of providing web content using the centralized web server model. Not many people in the organization have the technical skills or knowledge to set up a web server, but they have published their home page because of this model.

Earlier, we mentioned the benefits of using file sharing services such as NFS and name services such as DNS to enable users to seamlessly access resources that are centralized and easily managed. Using the powerful combination of file sharing services and name services, you can give users the capability to publish web information in an intranet without creating a system and network administration nightmare for yourself.

Without the benefit of centralized file sharing and name services, the web information that each individual in the organization creates tends to be fragmented and spread across the organization in a non-uniform manner that introduces many administration problems.

In the "personal server" model, users install, configure, and maintain intranet services from their personal desktop system. If you take the "personal server" model and multiply it by the number of people in the organization who need to publish web information in an intranet, you quickly understand that is extremely difficult and costly to manage intranet services that are not centralized.

A better model is to set up web services on a single, corporate server, instead of hundreds of personal servers in a network, and configure access to the web directories from the user's home directory using file sharing and name services, as shown in Figure 16-2.

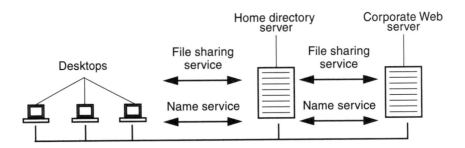

**Figure 16-2** Centralized Web Services

In this model, a single machine, the corporate Web server, accesses hundreds of home directories across the network using file sharing and name services. The web service on the single corporate web server serves all of the user's home pages, stored as `public_html` in the user's home directory. The physical location of the user's home directory doesn't matter in this model – the file sharing and name service handles the work of locating and accessing these resources for you.

## Summary

In this chapter, we've shown how intranet web services can be used to enable communication within an organization. More importantly, we introduced a server-centric model of providing web services that promotes centralized administration by leveraging other intranet services. In the next chapter, we'll describe how to select, install, and configure the software that enables web services—the web server.

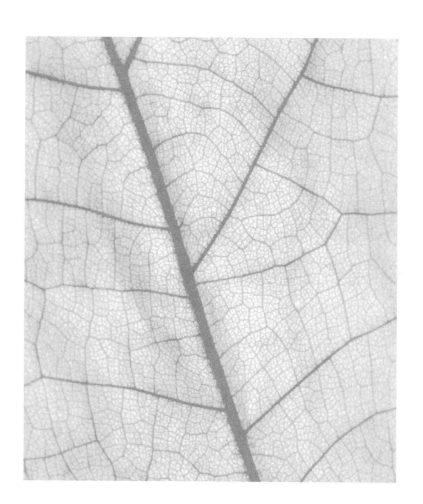

# CHAPTER 17

# Setting Up Web Services

I n this chapter, we'll describe the software used to implement web services in an intranet. Because both public domain or commercial web server software is available, we'll explain the benefits of each of the more popular packages to help you identify the features you need and select the web server that is right for your intranet. We'll also show you how to install and configure the Apache and Netscape FastTrack Web server software, since they each provide a good example of the administrative differences you will encounter using public domain and commercial web servers.

## Choosing a Web Server

Web services are implemented using the Hyper Text Transfer Protocol (HTTP) service. This functionality is provided by web server software, also known as web servers. There are many public domain and commercial web servers[1] available for you to use in an intranet. Generally speaking, commercial web server software is easier to install and administer than public domain software, and it offers enhanced functionality that is not found in the public domain, such as support for secure web transactions. In this section, we'll describe several popular public domain and commercial web servers to help you choose one that meets your needs.

---

1. For a list of servers, visit http://www.yahoo.com/Computers_and_Internet/ Software/Internet/World_Wide_Web/Servers/.

### Public Domain Web Server Software

The following web server software is in the public domain, and it can used in an intranet without having to pay licensing fees.

- NCSA

  This web server is available for Solaris and other UNIX operating environments and provides basic HTTP services. To obtain this software, visit the NCSA web site (http://hoohoo.ncsa.uiuc.edu/). An unsupported version is also available for Windows.

- W3C HTTPD (formerly know as CERN)

  The W3C HTTPD software provides generic HTTP services like the NCSA server. It is particularly well suited for an intranet because it adds proxy services that provide access for users inside the firewall to external web sites. It also supports caching, which improves access times and reduces network loads (see *Firewall and Proxy Services* on page 37).The server runs on most UNIX operating environments, including Solaris. To obtain this software, visit the W3C web site (http://www.w3.org/pub/WWW/Daemon/).

- Apache

  For simple document serving purposes, the Apache[2] server is an excellent choice. This server software is gaining popularity in the intranet, because it is compatible with the NCSA configuration files, making it easy for NCSA installations to upgrade to Apache. Even though it is public domain software, Apache has most of the features of the commercial web servers, such as caching and proxy services. Among the commercial features the Apache server lacks is a user-friendly administrative interface, and advanced security features such as support for the Secure Socket Layer (SSL). The server runs on most UNIX operating environments, including Solaris. To obtain this software, visit the Apache web site (http://www.apache.org/).

---

2. For more information, visit http://www.apache.org/docs/FAQ.html.

### Commercial Web Server Software

The following commercial web server software products are available for a cost from the listed companies. These Web servers provide a number of features that add value, such as better administrative interfaces, better security, and better support.

- Netscape Communications Server (NCS)

  The NCS web server software is a popular choice for Solaris and other UNIX operating environments because it offers extensive access control capabilities. For example, the NCS software enables you to easily perform the following administration tasks:

  - Remap URLs
  - Access server logs

  *Special Capabilities*

  - Enables secure web transactions

  This capability is especially useful for applications dealing with sensitive information, such as payroll, employee benefits, and so on. The NCS software encrypts the data that is exchanged between the web server and web client, and also encrypts the communications channel that is established between the client and server.

  *Setup*

  The NCS software uses a Netscape Navigator browser-based configuration program. This is typical of commercial web server software, in that an easy-to-use GUI is provided for configuration and administration purposes.

  *Available platforms*

  The server runs on Solaris and other UNIX operating environments. It is also available for Windows NT.

- Microsoft Internet Information Server (IIS)

  IIS is bundled in the Windows NT operating environment, version 4.0. It is not included in the Windows 95 operating environment.

  *Special Capabilities*

  The IIS web server software enables you to perform these administrative tasks:

  - Add access
  - Disable access
  - Access server logs

  *Setup*
  The IIS software is configured automatically at installation time.

- Netscape Communications FastTrack Server

  If you intend restrict access to web services based on either the login name/password or the IP or domain name and want to have an easy user interface for administration purposes, the Netscape FastTrack server is a good choice. The Netscape FastTrack server uses a web browser-based interface for administration and configuration (see "Installing the Netscape FastTrack Server – Solaris" on page 266.) If you don't care about the details of Web administration, the FastTrack Server is an easy-to-use, entry-level Web server designed to let anyone create and manage a web site.

- Netscape Communications Enterprise Server

  If you intend to use secure-authentication, the Netscape's Enterprise Server is a good choice. It can communicate with a web client using Secure Sockets Layer and certificates, providing a reasonable level security using an encrypted channel. The Netscape Enterprise Server can authenticate web clients on the basis of public-key certificates. This cryptographically-strong form of user authentication eliminates the task of maintaining access control rights to server resources, and enables users to access multiple servers without having to remember multiple user name and password combinations. The Netscape Enterprise Server can be used to provide access to employee records, salary, HR records, and other sensitive information using a web service.

### Commercial Web Server Software Benefits

Commercial web server software enables you to perform administration tasks from a remote computer, using a web browser or similar GUI. None of the public domain web server software offers this capability. For this reason alone, the web server software from companies such as Netscape and Microsoft offer a unique administrative advantage: ease-of-use. You don't have to perform error-prone tasks such as editing configuration files by hand, for example. To summarize, the value of commercial Web server software is not only in the enhanced capabilities they offer such as secure HTTP, but in the cost savings brought upon by easy-to-use administration tools.

In order to perform administrative tasks remotely, the web server software first authenticates you before allowing you access and modifying configuration information.

Here are some of the administrative capabilities provided by commercial web servers:

- HTTP load balancing

You can specify to which server you want to serve a specified URL by mapping URLs to servers. You can do this without having to make any changes to the web server aliases stored in the name space.

* Access Control

  You can restrict access to the information "tree" on the web server based on any one of the following client attributes:

  * IP address
  * IP address class
  * Domain name
  * Machine name
  * User name

  You can also restrict access to Common Gateway Interface (CGI) functionality.

* Monitoring

  Monitoring controls enables you to trim or reduce the size of web access logs, schedule purges of the logs based on how much they grow, and so on.

  More importantly, you can gather statistics on how your site is being accessed. For example, you can determine which pages are more frequently accessed, and see who is accessing the information. This capability can be invaluable in helping to make decisions regarding site organization, effectiveness, and so on.

## Installing the Apache Web Server – Solaris

First, let's look at Apache, a public domain HTTP server. The installation and configuration of Apache requires some work on your part, but in return you get the opportunity to learn about the details of running a web server.

*Task Overview*

Here is an overview of the tasks required to install an Apache server for Solaris.

* Download the Apache software distribution
* Edit the configuration file and compile the Apache software
* Configure the Apache server
* Start and verify the Apache server

Each of these tasks is described in this section.

*Prerequisites*

You must have a C compiler installed on your system to compile the Apache software.

### Downloading the Apache Software Distribution

Apache[3] 1.1.3 is available in binary format for multiple platforms. Information[4] about how to compile, install, and configure the Apache server is also available online.

### Compiling the Apache Software

1.   **Become super-user.**

2.   **Unpack the source distribution.**

```
# cd /opt
# zcat apache_1.1.3.tar.Z | tar xfv -
```

3.   **Edit the file used to build the Apache server executables.**
     Enable the compilers and auxiliary flags for Solaris.

```
# cd apache_1.1.3/src
# vi Configuration
```

You can also add modules to your build. For now take the default configuration. If you want to add features such as proxy services later, you can enable the optional module(s) and rebuild the server executables.

4.   **Run the configuration script.**

```
# ./Configure
```

The script will determine your system-type, and it will automatically generate the appropriate `Makefile` and configuration files.

3.   Solaris binaries for SPARC and x86 can be found in
     ftp://www.apache.org/apache/dist/binaries/solaris_2.5.
4.   See http://www.apache.org/docs/.

**5.** Compile the executables.

```
# /usr/ccs/bin/make
```

The server executables are now built. The next step is to configure the
server.

### Installing the Apache Server

Perform this procedure if you wish to install the Apache server manually. If you
prefer, you can run the Apache setup script described on page 262.

**1.** Create the Apache installation directory.

```
# mkdir /opt/apache
```

**2.** Change the directory to the Apache source directory.

```
# cd /opt/apache_1.1.3
```

**3.** Copy the configuration files to the installation directory.

```
# cp -rp conf cgi-bin htdocs icons logs src/httpd support /opt/apache
```

**4.** Change the directory to the Apache configuration directory.

```
# cd /opt/apache/conf
```

**5.** Copy the distribution (-dist) files and edit these fields.

```
httpd.conf - "ServerRoot"
srm.conf - "DocumentRoot"
access.conf - "Directory"
```

### Apache Setup Script

Example 17-1 is provided as a convenient way to install and configure the Apache HTTP server after you have compiled it. The script copies the binaries, icons, and directories to the installation area. It also edits the sample configuration files, and it creates new files suitable for initial use.

**Example 17-1** apachesetup.sh **Apache Setup Script**

```
#!/bin/sh
[ -d cgi-bin -a -d conf -a -d htdocs -a -d icons -a -d logs ] || {
  echo "cd to the apache directory before running $0"
  exit 1
}

adir=/opt/apache
[ -d $adir ] || {
  mkdir $adir
}
cp -rp conf cgi-bin htdocs icons logs src/httpd support $adir
cd $adir/conf
sed -e "s,^<Directory .*>,<Directory $adir>," access.conf-dist >
access.conf
sed -e "s,^DocumentRoot .*,DocumentRoot $adir/htdocs," \
    -e "s,#Alias .*,Alias /icons/ $adir/icons/," \
    -e "s,#ScriptAlias .*,ScriptAlias /chi-bin/ $adir/cgi-bin/," \
    srm.conf-dist > srm.conf
sed -e "s,^ServerRoot .*,ServerRoot $adir," \
    -e "s,Group #-1,Group nobody," \
        httpd.conf-dist > httpd.conf
```

### Verifying the Apache Server

Perform this procedure to verify that the Apache server is properly installed and configured.

**1.   Start the Apache server process.**

```
# /opt/apache/httpd -d /opt/apache
```

**2.   Launch a web browser, and type in the following URL.**

```
http://localhost/
```

The Apache test page is displayed.

### Starting the Apache Server at Boot Time

To start Apache automatically at boot time, you can use the script shown in Example 17-2.

**Example 17-2** www Apache Server Startup Script

```
#!/sbin/sh
WWWHOME=/opt/apache

killproc() {               # kill the named process(es)
  pid=`cat ${WWWHOME}/logs/httpd.pid`
  [ "$pid" != "" ] && kill $pid
}

case $1 in
'start')
        echo "Starting WWW services."
        ${WWWHOME}/httpd -d ${WWWHOME}
        ;;
'stop')
        killproc httpd
        ;;
*)
        echo "usage: /etc/init.d/www {start|stop}"
        ;;
esac
```

To use this script:

1.  **Place a copy in the** /etc/init.d **directory.**
    Name the file www.

2.  **Create hard links to the run level 3 startup directory.**

```
# ln /etc/init.d/www /etc/rc3.d/K40wwww
# ln /etc/init.d/www /etc/rc3.d/S40www
```

The Apache server now automatically starts after any reboot.

## Configuring the Apache Server

Now that the web server is installed and running, you need to configure it with the following types of information:

- Server HTTP port(s)
- Webmaster e-mail address
- Base document directory
- Total number of concurrent connections allowed
- Clients allowed or denied access to the server

We'll briefly describe the configuration files used by the Apache server in this section. By default, these files are stored in the /opt/apache/conf directory.

For more information on how to use the parameters found in these files, visit the Apache web site (http://www.apache.org/docs/).

### The httpd.conf *File*

This file contains the server configuration information, and you can specify values for any of the following server parameters:

- Log files and their formats
- Server type—standalone or using the inetd process
- Server HTTP port(s); the default is 80
- Webmaster e-mail address
- Server base document directory
- Number of concurrent connections allowed

### The access.conf *File*

This file enables you to control how the server is accessed. In this file, you can perform the following configuration activities:

- Specify cgi-bin directories and permissions (see *The Common Gateway Interface* on page 279)
- Allow or deny client access to specified directories
- Allow or deny the server to follow symbolic links

### The `srm.conf` *File*

This file is used to define the structure of the documents stored on the Web server. You can use this file to control the behavior of the web server when a directory is visited by a web browser.

For example, if a directory is specified in a URL, the directory contents are displayed. If a file named `index.html` exists in the directory, it will be rendered by the web browser if it is an HTML file. The behavior of the `index.html` file name is configured using the directive `DirectoryIndex` in the `srm.conf` file, as shown below:

```
# DirectoryIndex: Name of the file or files to use as a pre-written HTML
# directory index.  Separate multiple entries with spaces.

DirectoryIndex index.html
```

You can map the name of the directory used to store user home pages with the `UseDir` directive:

```
# UserDir: The name of the directory which is appended onto a user's home
# directory if a ~user request is recieved.

UserDir public_html
```

The `public_html` directory is created in the user home directory, and populated with HTML pages. The user home page is then accessed using the following URL format:

```
http://web-server.domain/~user-login/
```

Directives[5] for icon mapping based on types and files to ignore can also be defined in the `srm.conf` file.

---

5.    For a comprehensive list, see the configurable directives documented in
      http://www.apache.org/docs/directives.html.

### *Adding Documents to the Server*

Now that the server is running, you can add documents to the server. By default, all documents are stored in the /opt/apache/htdocs directory. For example, to access the document /opt/apache/htdocs/mydoc.html on the web server, use the following URL:

```
http://web-server/mydoc.html
```

To access the document /opt/apache/htdocs/mydir/mydoc.html on the web server, use the following URL:

```
http://web-server/mydir/mydoc.html
```

You can map files in a directory to a specified URL using aliases. For example, you may have a directory full of documents in the /opt/sales/html directory. To map this directory to a different area on the web server, use the srm.conf file:

```
# Aliases: Add here as many aliases as you need (with no limit). The format is
# Alias fakename realname

Alias /sales/ /opt/sales/html/
```

Now, the /opt/sales/html directory can be accessed on the server by simply using the following URL:

```
http://web-server/sales
```

## Installing the Netscape FastTrack Server – Solaris

As you would expect from a commercial product, the Netscape FastTrack Server is much easier to install, configure, and administer than the Apache server. It uses a combination of web forms, CGI programs, JavaScript, and online help in a web browser environment to streamline server installation and administration.

*Task Overview*

Here is an overview of the tasks required to install a Netscape FastTrack Server for Solaris.

- Download the Netscape FastTrack Server software
- Prepare information needed by the server software installation program
- Run the command-line installation program
- Install the server using Netscape Navigator

Each of these tasks is described in this section.

*Prerequisites*

The `ns-setup` program is used to install the Netscape FastTrack Server software on your system. The server itself is installed using the Netscape Navigator web browser – be sure that it is available for use on your system.

Before you run the `ns-setup` program, be prepared to answer questions about the installation. You will be prompted for information about the system on which you wish to install the server, as well as for options for setting up administrative access to the server. Specifically, you have to specify the following:

- The server's fully-qualified host name

    The host name must including the domain name, as shown in this example.

---

```
web-server.company.com
```

---

- An administration port number

    By default, the installation program randomly selects a port number to use for administrative purposes. You can specify a port number, but don't use a number under 1000, as they are reserved for use by the system.

- The user ID (UID) to run the administration server program

    The default UID is root.

- An administrator user login name and password

    The default administrator login is `admin` (you must specify a password). This account is used by the administration server for authentication purposes.

- A list of host names and IP addresses from which you intend to administer the server

  Here, you specify the host names from which you intend to run the Netscape Navigator Web browser to perform administrative operations. Only the hosts you specify are authorized to log onto the Netscape FastTrack Server.

- The command used to invoke the Netscape Navigator server in your environment

### Downloading the Netscape FastTrack Server Software

**1. Obtain the software distribution.**
Obtain the Netscape Server software from the Netscape Web site (http://home.mcom.com/comprod/mirror/server_download.html/). You can complete a server test drive license agreement online that entitles you to evaluate the software for 60 days.

**2. Unpack the distribution.**
An example is shown below.

```
# cd /tmp
# gzip -d ft-20-export.sparc-sun-solaris2.4.tar.gz
# tar xfv ft-20-export.sparc-sun-solaris2.4.tar
```

### Installing the Netscape FastTrack Server Software

**1. Become super-user.**
You must run the installation program using the `root` UID.

**2.   Run the installation program.**

```
#  ./ns-setup
```

The installation program prompts you for the information described earlier using a series of menus. Upon successful completion, the program starts Netscape Navigator, and presents you with a login window. An example login window is shown below.

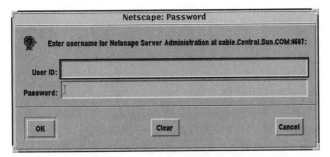

**3.   Enter your Netscape FastTrack Server administrator login and password.** The server authenticates you, and the Netscape Server Selector page is displayed.

### Installing the Netscape FastTrack Server

You can easily install web services using Netscape FastTrack Server GUI. The task of installing a web server is greatly simplified using the familiar Netscape Navigator web browser interface, as shown below.

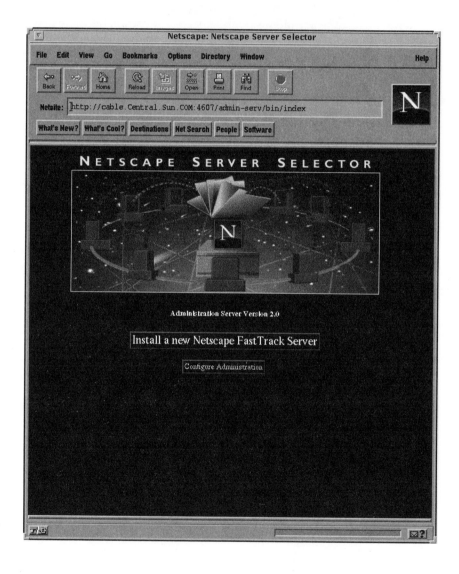

**1.** Click on **Install a new Netscape FastTrack Server.**
The server installation form is displayed. An example is shown below.

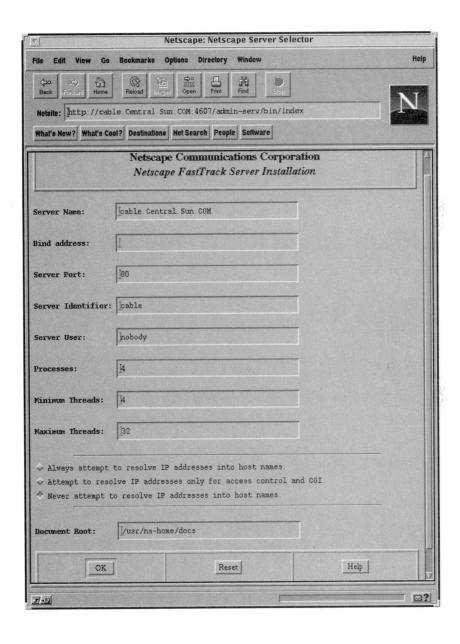

**2. Accept the defaults, and click OK.**

The server is created, and the page is updated to show the new server. An example is shown below.

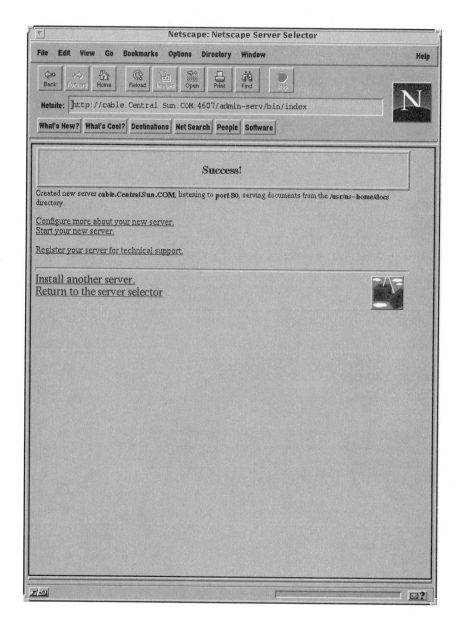

**3.**   **Click Start your new server.**

A dialog confirming that the server has started up is displayed, as shown below.

4.    **Click OK to dismiss the dialog.**

The Netscape Server page is displayed, and the new server appears in the server list. An example is shown below.

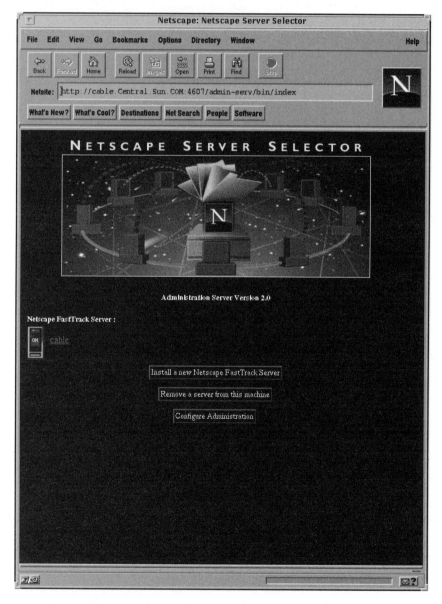

The Netscape FastTrack Server is now ready for use.

## Post-Installation Tasks

### Enabling Users to Publish Home Pages

After installing the web server, verify that users' home directories are available to the server using file sharing and name services (see *Setting Up File Sharing and Printing Services* on page 143 and *Name Services* on page 159). This enables users to easily publish information such as home pages using the web server.

If home directories are accessed in a consistent manner within the name space, then all the home directories in the intranet can be accessed from the web server. Here is an example of a consistent home directory path:

---

`/home/`*`user-login`*

---

Access is enabled using a file sharing service such as NFS and a fixed naming service such as NIS and AutoFS.

To publish HTML pages using the web server, users create the `public_html` directory within their home directory. This directory and its contents should be world-readable, but writable only by the user. In this directory, they can store the `index.html` page, other HTML pages, and related information they want to publish.

A user's home page is accessed from within the intranet using the following URL format:

---

`http://`*`web-server.domain`*`/~`*`user-login`*`/`

---

The web server specified in this URL automatically mounts the user's home directory using file sharing and name services, and it serves the HTML pages and other data stored in the user's `public_html` directory to the requestor.

In this manner, the home pages for all users in the intranet are published using a single web server. You can accomplish this using a consistent name space, as indicated by the universal home directory access path, `/home/`*`user-login`*. A person searching for a user's home page is guaranteed access using a centralized web server and a consistent name space. The only information that is needed to construct the URL and to visit the user's home page is the web server name and the user login.

This also enables you to write scripts to perform routine administrative tasks, such as looking up user information.

## Summary

Both public domain and commercial web servers can be used to provide robust and reliable Web services in an intranet. While freely-available web server software is appealing to many organizations because of the cost savings it brings, commercial software packages provide a compelling set of features that can't be easily ignored either. Ultimately, choosing a web server depends on a number of factors, including the economic realities of your organization. Either way, you won't be disappointed by the choices that are available to you.

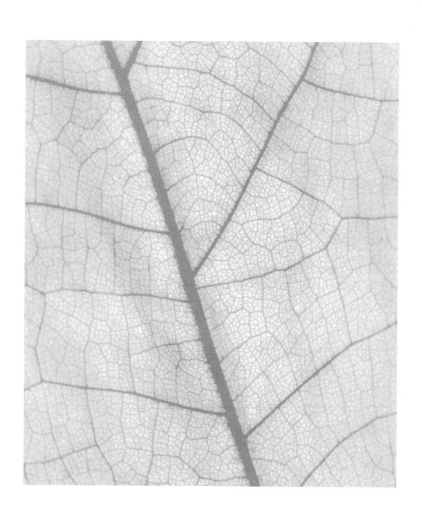

# CHAPTER
# 18

# The Common Gateway Interface

## What is the Common Gateway Interface?

The common gateway interface (CGI) is a web standard for interfacing with external applications. CGI works like a bridge, accessing data stored in legacy systems for use in an open, standards-based web environment. For example, a web browser can start a report generation program residing on an HTTP server, and the report is formatted in HTML and returned to the browser for viewing. This capability provides the potential for database queries and other types of access from any desktop capable of running a web browser, and not just specially configured client systems running a proprietary software.

CGI is an good tool for information gathering and processing activities using the popular and easy-to-use web browser GUI. Here are some examples of how to use CGI:

- Surveys

- Online registration

- Data entry

- Database queries

Databases that once had stringent client-side requirements have found a new life on the web. With CGI, information processing activities such as data entry and report generation that once required special interfaces can now be performed using the ubiquitous web browser interface. In fact, CGI often enables cost-savings because of the rapid application development capabilities inherent to the web. For example, a data entry form can be easily constructed with just a few lines of HTML, and the form is ready for immediate display and testing in the Web browser. Free public domain software, such as the Apache HTTP server software and the Perl programming language, have also greatly reduced the development costs for many organizations implementing intranets. When contrasted with expensive, proprietary software products from commercial vendors that offer similar functionality, web technologies such as CGI and HTTP easily win out.

### Why Use CGI?

There are many immediately useful applications of CGI for your organization. For example, you can construct a CGI program to interface into an employee phone book database, and enable any intranet user to search and retrieve information from their desktop using a web browser. Since the user interface is a web browser, users can choose the platform they want — be it a PC, UNIX, JavaStation, or a Mac desktop — it doesn't matter. Web technologies eliminate the need to develop custom application interfaces for each platform.

CGI is versatile, and it has many uses. For example, you can write a CGI program to talk to a database using existing interfaces or you can construct a CGI interface to modify the name service database maps stored in the NIS directory service. By adding login authentication, you can enable users to perform system administration activities such as adding users, modifying desktop configurations, configuring printers, all using the web from any remote desktop — be it PC, UNIX, JavaStation, or Mac.

### CGI Limitations

CGI places most of the information processing burden on the HTTP server. Beyond activities such as submitting queries and rendering the resulting HTML, the web browser client does little of the work. HTTP servers can quickly be overloaded executing CGI programs, with users suffering from slow response times. If the network is busy, response time also suffers. Constructing custom CGI programs also requires a certain level of programming expertise (writing CGI programs is usually easier than programming in other environments, however).

### Enabling CGI Programs on the Server

CGI programs reside in a special location on the web server. This enables the web server to execute the program rather than just display the contents to a requesting client web browser.

### The cgi-bin *Directory*

This directory is usually named cgi-bin, and it is enabled in the srm.conf configuration file using the directive "ScriptAlias" (see *Setting Up Web Services* on page 255 for more information). If you installed the Apache HTTP server using the provided script, the cgi-bin directory is /opt/apache/cgi-bin and is enabled in the /opt/apache/config/srm.conf configuration file using the following directive.

```
"ScriptAlias /cgi-bin/ /opt/apache/cgi-bin/
```

## How CGI Works

A CGI program behaves like any other program. The main difference between a regular program and a CGI program is that the CGI program does not have command line input (arguments). The input is constructed using the forms capability of the web browser, and it is passed to the CGI program available on the server. The CGI program reads the input from the HTML form and sends the output (written to stdout) to the web browser. Usually, the output is in HTML format. This process is illustrated in Figure 18-1.

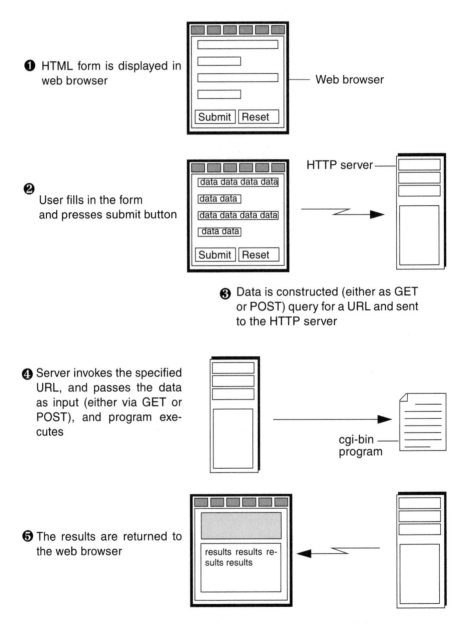

❶ HTML form is displayed in web browser

Web browser

❷ User fills in the form and presses submit button

HTTP server

❸ Data is constructed (either as GET or POST) query for a URL and sent to the HTTP server

❹ Server invokes the specified URL, and passes the data as input (either via GET or POST), and program executes

cgi-bin program

❺ The results are returned to the web browser

results results results results

**Figure 18-1** Example – HTML Form Processing Using CGI

## CGI Uses

So far we've talked about how CGI is used to process HTML forms. Though this is a common application, CGI can be used for almost any type of data processing activity. Here are other examples of how to use CGI:

- Data collection

  This can be submitting a database entry on the server, for example.

- Data access

  An example is displaying plain text (or HTML) as a result of a database query.

- Referral service

  This is where the client request is forwarded to another URL using the "Location:" tag.

- Interactive editing

  After submitting a completed form, a follow-up form is provided based on the initially submitted values.

- Image mapping

  The user clicks on an image, and a URL is loaded based on the region of the image where the user chose to click.

Remember that the CGI computing work is done on the server. Since CGI programs are accessed on the server, you can use the server to perform optional user authentication, and control the use of CGI functionality. The only work done on the client is the rendering and viewing of the HTML output. Complicated computing tasks can be customized (based on user requests) and performed on the server, leaving the web browser for simple viewing tasks.

## Using CGI Programs

### The GET *Method*

There are two methods to send input to a CGI program, specifically GET and POST. Let's look at the GET method first. The GET method gathers its input from the QUERY_STRING environment variable. QUERY_STRING is defined as anything that follows the first ? character in the URL. To understand how this works, we'll use examples from the test-cgi script found in the Apache HTTP server distribution.

The following URL is an example of fixed input to a CGI program.

```
<A HREF="/cgi-bin/test-cgi?entry=value">get query</A>
```

Let's say that this link appears in the file `mytest.html`. After loading this file in a web browser and accessing the link, the following results are displayed.

```
CGI/1.0 test script report:

argc is 0. argv is .

SERVER_SOFTWARE = Apache/1.1.1
SERVER_NAME = myweb.mycomany.COM
GATEWAY_INTERFACE = CGI/1.1
SERVER_PROTOCOL = HTTP/1.0
SERVER_PORT = 80
REQUEST_METHOD = GET
HTTP_ACCEPT = image/gif, image/x-xbitmap, image/jpeg, image/pjpeg,
*/*
PATH_INFO =
PATH_TRANSLATED =
SCRIPT_NAME = /cgi-bin/test-cgi
QUERY_STRING = entry=value
REMOTE_HOST = myweb
REMOTE_ADDR = xxx.xxx.xxx.xxx
REMOTE_USER =
AUTH_TYPE =
CONTENT_TYPE =
CONTENT_LENGTH =
```

This is a list of the environment variables[1] available to CGI programs on the HTTP server. This should give you a good understanding of the types of information available to your CGI program for parsing and processing. Specifically, the following entry is particularly important.

```
"QUERY_STRING = entry=value"
```

1.  A full list of environment variables available to a CGI program can be obtained using http://hoohoo.ncsa.uiuc.edu/cgi/env.html/.

This is the fixed input we originally submitted to the `test-cgi` CGI program, which is used as the standard input to the CGI program. To provide variable input to a CGI program, we can use the forms mechanism in HTML. This example shows how to construct variable input to a CGI program using HTML.

```
<FORM METHOD=GET ACTION="/cgi-bin/test-cgi">
<INPUT TYPE="text"   NAME="entry">
<INPUT TYPE="submit" VALUE="submit this field">
</FORM>
```

Figure 18-2 shows how the HTML appears when rendered in a web browser.

**Figure 18-2** Example – Simple Web Browser Form

After entering the string `myval` in the entry field and pressing the button, this is the result sent to the CGI program:

```
"QUERY_STRING = entry=myval"
```

### CGI Program Example – Perl

To illustrate different CGI techniques and concepts, we'll use a CGI program using the Perl programming language. Perl[2] is a popular language used for CGI programming because it handles string processing particularly well, it's fast, it's available for most platforms (including Windows), and it's free. We'll assume rudimentary Perl knowledge for the example used in this chapter. We'll start with the Perl script shown in Example 18-1.

2.  To learn more about Perl, see Programming Perl, by Larry Wall, ISBN: 0-937175-64-1, and see the Perl FAQ at http://scwww.ucs.indiana.edu/FAQ/Perl/index.html.

**Example 18-1** `getquery.pl` **Perl CGI Script**

```perl
#!/usr/local/bin/perl
%query = &get_query;
@key = keys %query;

print "Content-type:text/html\n\n";
print "entry=$query{'entry'}";
sub get_query {
    local($query_string);
    local($method) = $ENV{'REQUEST_METHOD'};

    if ($method eq 'GET') {
  $query_string = $ENV{'QUERY_STRING'};
    }
    else {
  $query_string = "Error in CGI form";
    }
    return () unless $query_string;
    return &parse_params($query_string)
        if $query_string =~ /=/;
}
sub unescape {
    local($todecode) = @_;
    $todecode =~ tr/+/ /;# pluese to spaces
    $todecode =~ s/%([0-9A-Ha-h]{2})/pack("c",hex($1))/ge;
    return $todecode;
}
sub parse_params {
    local($tosplit) = @_;
    local(@pairs) = split('&',$tosplit);
    local($param,$value,%parameters);
    foreach(@pairs) {
  ($param,$value) = split('=');
  $param = &unescape($param);
  $value = &unescape($value);
  if($parameters{$param}) {
      $parameters{$param} .= "$;$value";
  }
  else {
      $parameters{$param} = $value;
  }
    }
    return %parameters;
}
1;
```

### *The* POST *Method*

The GET method we described earlier is ideal for simple input to CGI programs. Recall that the GET method relies on the QUERY_STRING environment variable to pass input to the CGI program. However, reading input using environment variables such as QUERY_STRING has input length limitations on some systems. To address this shortcoming, CGI uses the POST method, which is a more flexible mechanism for handling input. This method is easy-to-use — the same HTML form constructs used in GET methods can be used unmodified in POST methods. To use POST methods, the CGI program needs to be constructed differently. Unlike the GET method where input is read from an environment variable, the POST method reads its input from the standard input (stdin).

This presents a challenge in that specifying the end of standard input for the CGI program can be difficult. Using the POST method, the CGI program is notified of the number of bytes sent to standard input using an environment variable. The server does not send an end of file (EOF) code at the end of the data. Instead, the environment variable CONTENT_LENGTH is used to determine how much data needs to be read from the standard input. Reading the right length of data is the CGI program's responsibility.

This example shows how to construct variable input to a CGI program using HTML and the POST method.

```
<FORM METHOD=POST ACTION="/cgi-bin/test-cgi">
 <INPUT TYPE="text"   NAME="entry">
 <INPUT TYPE="submit" VALUE="submit this field">
 </FORM>
```

All the environment variables mentioned above are still accessible using both CGI methods (GET and POST). The REQUEST_METHOD environment variable describes the type of CGI method used. Using this variable, we'll extend our Perl CGI script to dynamically adopt the CGI method (GET or POST) and process information using either method, as shown in Example 18-2.

**Example 18-2** getquery2.pl **Perl CGI Script**

```perl
#!/usr/local/bin/perl

sub get_query {
    local($query_string);
    local(@lines);
    local($method) = $ENV{'REQUEST_METHOD'};
    if ($method eq 'GET') {# fetch the query from the environment
    $query_string = $ENV{'QUERY_STRING'};
    }
    elsif ($method eq 'POST') { # fetch the query from stdin
    read (STDIN,$query_string,$ENV{'CONTENT_LENGTH'});
    }
    else {
    $query_string = "Error in CGI form";
    }
    return () unless $query_string;
    return &parse_params($query_string) if $query_string =~ /=/;
    return &parse_keywordlist($query_string);
}
sub unescape {
    local($todecode) = @_;
    $todecode =~ tr/+/ /;# plus two spaces
    $todecode =~ s/%([0-9A-Ha-h]{2})/pack("c",hex($1))/ge;
    return $todecode;
}
sub parse_keywordlist {
    local($tosplit) = @_;
    $tosplit = &unescape($tosplit);
    $tosplit =~ tr/+/ /;
    local(@keywords) = split(/\s+/,$tosplit); #split ws
    return @keywords;
}
```

```
sub parse_params {
   local($tosplit) = @_;
   local(@pairs) = split('&',$tosplit);
   local($param,$value,%parameters);
   foreach(@pairs) {
($param,$value) = split('=');
$param = &unescape($param);
$value = &unescape($value);
if($parameters{$param}) {
    $parameters{$param} .= "$;$value";
}
else {
    $parameters{$param} = $value;
}
   }
   return %parameters;
}
```

## Using HTML Forms for CGI Input

So far, we've shown only a very simple HTML form with a single entry field and button. You can build much more versatile HTML forms to collect input for a CGI program that employ the following user interface (UI) components:

- Text entry fields
- Check boxes
- Radio buttons
- Scrolling lists with single and multiple selections
- Option menus

To specify a UI component, use the `INPUT TYPE` directive[3]. This example shows how to specify a text entry field for input.

```
<INPUT TYPE="text" NAME="xxx">
<INPUT TYPE="password" NAME="xxx">
```

3. For more information on HTML form directives, see http://www.ncsa.uiuc.edu/SDG/Software/Mosaic/Docs/fill-out-forms/overview.html/.

### *The* `password` *and* `hidden` *Input Types*

Each input type has optional attributes that control its display in the web browser, such as size, placement, and other layout characteristics. Two of these attributes are worth noting, `type=password` and `type=hidden`. The `password` attribute hides the text and displays an * character for each character typed in that field, which is a useful feature for assigning individual logins to specific areas, for example. The `type=hidden` attribute does not display any visible characters on the web browser, but it allows input fields to be attached with additional values. These hidden fields are passed along with other name value pairs, but are not visible on the form. The CGI program can detect and process them, just as it does with other input fields.

## Summary

As we mentioned earlier, a form that produces input for a CGI program can also produce a CGI form as an output, thus providing a level of interaction between the user and the remote system. However, CGI programs *do not retain state between sessions.*

A common way to retain state is to use hidden fields. A CGI program can embed a state indicator as a hidden field in its output, and detect the state of the hidden field in subsequent sessions. We'll show how this is done in the next chapter.

# CHAPTER 19

# Using the Common Gateway Interface

In the previous chapter, we looked at the technical side of CGI programming. We covered how to use variables in a CGI program, and how to parse the input generated by an HTML form for processing using CGI. In this chapter, we'll use examples to show the practical application of CGI in the intranet.

## Using CGI in the Intranet

Let's reiterate the reasons why CGI is an important technology for the intranet.

- CGI is flexible and provides dynamic content

- CGI acts as a gateway to access legacy data using the Web

- User interfaces for data access and online surveys can be quickly prototyped, tested, and deployed independent of the legacy data format

For these reasons, CGI is ideal for quickly building customized applications designed to run in the familiar web browser environment. It is a cost-effective way to provide users with access to legacy information using the easy-to-use and ubiquitous web browser interface.

### CGI Applications

CGI covers a broad span of functionality and utility in an intranet. For example, a CGI application can provide simple searching and lookup capabilities for an online employee database, or it can be extended to include advanced features, such as accessing and modifying employee records using secure interfaces.

Here are some other examples of how CGI can be used in the intranet:

- Monitor system activities
- Manage network resources
- Manage user accounts
- Access online catalogs
- Track inventory
- Order goods and services

As you can see from these examples, CGI can be used in a variety of settings, to provide a wide range of capabilities to a diverse end-user audience.

### CGI Benefits

Besides its usefulness in providing solutions to day-to-day business activities, CGI offers benefits to intranet administrators and end-users alike. Here are just a few of these benefits:

- User interfaces, programming logic, business records, and other information can be managed centrally on the HTTP server.

- All intranet users can access data and application functionality stored in legacy databases using a common web browser-based interface.

- CGI doesn't require you to rewrite or port applications—it uses native, published interfaces to information resources. For example, a CGI program can use structured query language (SQL) to access data stored in a legacy relational database, it can use the `ypmatch` command to access information stored in NIS.

- Data crunching can be performed on a powerful HTTP server, lifting the data-processing burden from client systems. Very little is required of the client, other than being capable of running a web browser and communicating over the network.

Now that we've covered the uses and benefits of CGI, let's delve into our example CGI application.

## CGI Example – Employee Phone List

To give you an idea of the effort that is required to write a CGI application, we'll start with a very simple example—an online phone list. We'll try to mimic the application development environment in most organizations by adding refinements to our CGI application, as often occurs when users request changes and enhancements to existing applications.

### *CGI Application Overview*

We'll develop the following components for our online phone list:

* Simple HTML-based query interface

* Perl-based CGI script

In our example, we'll use employee data that is stored in a flat ASCII text file. The HTML form is used to collect the query from the user, and the Perl script is used to process the query and return the results to the user (the script uses UNIX text-processing utilities for the sake of expediency and simplicity). Later, we'll look at an example of using more advanced techniques to retrieve network information using published interfaces.

### *Employee Data*

Let's say the phone list is stored in an ASCII text file using the following format.

```
Last, First        Login      Ph.Ext. Home Phone   Desktop     Office
--
Ordorica, Lou      lou        8459    542-3455     rockies     B450
Dasan, Vasanthan vasa         4354    232-5932     braves      2148
```

### *HTML Form*

We'll use the HTML code shown in Example 19-1 to create a form for looking up employee information.

**Example 19-1** Phone List Query – HTML Form Code

```
<FORM METHOD=POST ACTION="/~vasa/cgi-bin/phonebook">
To search the online phonebook,<br>
enter username  <INPUT TYPE="text" NAME="name">
 <INPUT TYPE="submit" VALUE="submit this field">
</FORM>
```

Figure 19-1 shows how the form is displayed in a web browser interface.

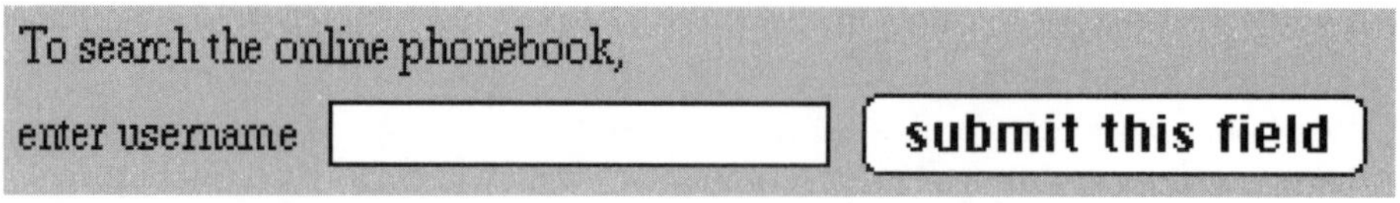

**Figure 19-1** Phone List Query – HTML Form Display

Now that we have a means of collecting input from the user, we need to look at how to process the query using CGI. Note that the CGI program associated with the form is specified in the first entry as /~vasa/cgi-bin/phonebook. Let's take a look at this CGI.

### CGI – Perl Script

The CGI specified as the action in our query is shown in Example 19-2. It is a script written in Perl, a popular language used for many CGIs. Perl has strong text processing capabilities that appeal to many CGI programmers, and we'll tap into this capability to handle the processing for our online phonelist.

**Example 19-2** phone.pl **Employee Phone List CGI**

```perl
#!/usr/local/bin/perl
$pl = "/usr/local/misc/phonelist";
# The following statement calls the getquery.pl Perl library
# described on page 286
require "getquery.pl";
%query = &get_query;

print "Content-type:text/html\n\n";
&dogrep($query{'name'});

sub dogrep {
    local ($user) = @_;

    open(GREP, "grep $user $pl|") || warn "Can't exec grep\n";
    while(<GREP>) {
        print;
    }
    close(GREP);
}
```

Our script receives the name value pairs as standard input, searches the ASCII employee database (`/usr/local/misc/phonelist`), and formats the results for display in the user's web browser.

Example 19-3 shows the simple results returned to the user.

**Example 19-3** Simple Phonelist Output

---

```
Ordorica, Lou lou 8459 542-3455 rockies B450
```

---

To provide results that are nicely formatted, we can modify the `dogrep` procedure in our Perl script, as shown in Example 19-4.

**Example 19-4** `phone2.pl` **Formatted Employee Phone List CGI**

---

```perl
sub dogrep {
    local ($user) = @_;

    open(GREP, "egrep $user $pl|") || warn "Can't exec grep\n";
    printf("<TABLE ALIGN=CENTER BORDER=1 CELLPADDING=2
CELLSPACING=2>");
    while(<GREP>) {
        ($ln, $rest) = split(/,/, $_);
        ($fn, $log, $op, $hp, $dt, $ol) = split(" ", $rest);
        printf("<TR><TD>First Name:</TD> <TD>%s</TD></TR>",$fn);
        printf("<TR><TD>Last Name:</TD> <TD>%s</TD></TR>",$ln);
        printf("<TR><TD>Login Name:</TD> <TD>%s</TD></TR>",$log);
        printf("<TR><TD>Office Phone:</TD> <TD>%s</TD></TR>",$op);
        printf("<TR><TD>Home Phone:</TD> <TD>%s</TD></TR>",$hp);
        printf("<TR><TD>Desktop Name:</TD> <TD>%s</TD></TR>",$dt);
        printf("<TR><TD>Office Location:</TD> <TD>%s</TD></TR>",$ol);
    }
    printf("</TABLE>");
    close(GREP);
}
```

---

Example 19-5 shows the table-formatted results returned to the user.

**Example 19-5** Table-Formatted Phone List Output

| | |
|---|---|
| First Name: | Lou |
| Last Name: | Ordorica |
| Login Name: | lou |
| Office Phone | 8459 |
| Home Phone: | 542-3455 |
| Desktop Name: | rockies |
| Office Location: | B450 |

Earlier we mentioned that flexibility is one of CGI's advantages—let's look at an example of this now. By providing different input to our CGI program, we can present different views of the employee data. For example, instead of returning the results of a query, we can provide users with the full list of employees. The CGI code that performs this function is shown in Example 19-6.

**Example 19-6** `phone3.pl` **Enhanced Employee Phone List CGI**

```perl
#!/usr/local//bin/perl
%query = &get_query;
@key = keys %query;
$pl = "/usr/local/misc/phonelist";

print "Content-type:text/html\n\n";
&showby($key[0]);


sub showby {
    local($by) = @_;

    if ($by =~ /firstname/) {
        $sortcmd = "sort -fb +1 -t\",\" $pl";
    }
    elsif ($by =~ /lastname/) {
        $sortcmd = "sort -fb $pl";
    }
    elsif ($by =~ /phone/) {
        $sortcmd = "sort -fb +3 $pl";
    }
    elsif ($by =~ /login/) {
        $sortcmd = "sort -fb +2 $pl";
    }
    elsif ($by =~ /machine/) {
        $sortcmd = "sort -fb +5 $pl";
    }
    elsif ($by =~ /office/) {
        $sortcmd = "sort -fb +6 $pl";
    }
    else {
        $sortcmd = "sort -fb $pl";
    }
    open(SORT, "$sortcmd|") || warn "Can't exec $sortcmd.\n";
    printf("<TABLE ALIGN=CENTER BORDER=1 CELLPADDING=2
CELLSPACING=2>");
    printf("<TR>");
    printf("<TH><A HREF=\"/cgi-bin/bk?firstname=1\">First
Name</A></TH>");
    printf("<TH><A HREF=\"/cgi-bin/bk?lastname=1\">Last
Name</A></TH>");
    printf("<TH><A HREF=\"/cgi-bin/bk?loginnmae=1\">Login
Name</A></TH>");
```

```
    printf("<TH>Office Phone</TH> <TH>Home Phone</TH> <TH>Desktop
Name</TH>");
    printf("<TH>Office Location</TH></TR>\n");
    while(<SORT>) {
        ($ln, $rest) = split(/,/, $_);
        ($fn, $log, $op, $hp, $dt, $ol) = split(" ", $rest);
        printf("<TR> <TD>%s</TD>", $fn);
        printf("<TD>%s</TD>", $ln);
        printf("<TD>%s</TD>", $log);
        printf("<TD>%s</TD>", $op);
        printf("<TD>%s</TD>", $hp);
        printf("<TD>%s</TD>", $dt);
        printf("<TD>%s</TD></TR>\n", $ol);
    }
    printf("</TABLE>");
    close(<SORT>);
}
```

Example 19-7 shows the table-formatted and sort-enabled results returned to the user.

**Example 19-7** Sort-Enabled Phone List Output

| First Name | Last Name | Login Name | Office Phone | Home Phone | Desktop Name | Office Location |
|---|---|---|---|---|---|---|
| Vasanthan | Dasan | vasa | 4354 | 232-5932 | braves | 2148 |
| Lou | Ordorica | lou | 8459 | 542-3455 | rockies | B450 |

The user changes the sort order of the table entries by clicking on either the First Name or Last Name column heading.

## Retaining State in CGI Programs

A limitation you may have noticed in our employee phone list CGI program is that it is useful only for simple transactions. Once the user obtains the results from the query, the transaction is essentially over—if someone wants to look up another name, they must start from scratch each time, for example.

More complex applications usually require more than a single transaction before the work is completed, and not all actions can be independent of previous actions. For example, someone might be perusing an online catalog and selecting items for purchase from multiple pages before actually submitting the order. In this case, we need a way to store the results of multiple queries in a web browsing session. This is called *retaining state* in CGI programs.

A problem arises in that the HTTP protocol upon which CGI is based is a stateless protocol, and it cannot retain the state in a web browsing session. To overcome this problem, we can use the *hidden field technique* in CGI.

### CGI Hidden Field Technique

This technique embeds queries using hidden fields in the results generated by a CGI, and it builds subsequent queries based on the embedded hidden query information. Since hidden fields are not displayed in a web browser, the state is retained across browser transactions in a manner that is transparent to the user.

The server-side CGI program uses the hidden field information stored in the CGI result. This field is not visible to the user, but it is part of the results sent to the browser, and it enables the CGI program to determine the state of the browser.

To show you how this works, let's look at an example. We'll use the hidden field technique in a CGI that performs system administration functions.

## CGI Example – Host Status

In this CGI, the user is prompted for a DNS domain. The list of hosts in the domain is returned to the user. From this list, the user chooses a host, and finds the status of the host's software and hardware. The CGI uses a hidden field to retain the state, or the domain in which the host resides, in the web browser session.

The HTML code shown in Example 19-8 prompts the user for a domain name (an example of the how this form is displayed in the web browser is shown in Figure 19-2).

**Example 19-8** Host Status Query – HTML Form Code

```
<FORM METHOD="POST" ACTION="/cgi-bin/admin">
<INPUT NAME=domainname TYPE=submit VALUE=Hosts>
<INPUT NAME=tasks TYPE=submit VALUE=Domain>
</FORM>
```

**Figure 19-2 Host Status Query – HTML Form Display**

Based on the domain name, the CGI lists the hosts in that domain. The user can then select a specific host, and find the status of that host's software and hardware. The context of the request from the HTML form is conveyed to the CGI program via the hidden fields.

When the user submits the form, the CGI generates the HTML form shown in Example 19-9 as the result. Notice how the context of the domain name is maintained using a hidden field.

**Example 19-9** Host Status Results – HTML Form Code

```
<FORM METHOD="POST" ACTION="/cgi-bin/admin">
<INPUT TYPE=hidden NAME=fordomain VALUE=rmtc.Central.Sun.COM>
<SELECT NAME=hostinfo SIZE=20>
<OPTION> host1
<OPTION> host2
....
</SELECT>
```

Figure 19-3 shows how the HTML form is displayed in the web browser, and you can see that our hidden field is not displayed.

**Figure 19-3** Host Status Results – HTML Form Display

The CGI used to generate these results is shown in Example 19-10.

**Example 19-10** host.pl **Host Status CGI**

```perl
#!/usr/local/bin/perl
%query = &get_query;
@key = keys %query;

print "Content-type:text/html\n\n<BODY>\n";
if (@key[0] eq "domainname") {
    $domain = $query{'domainname'};
    &form_begin("Hosts");
    print "<INPUT TYPE=hidden NAME=fordomain VALUE=$domain>\n";
    print "<SELECT NAME=hostinfo SIZE=20>\n";
    &gethostsbydomain($domain);
    print "</SELECT>";
    &form_end("List Hosts Information");
}
elsif ((@key[0] eq "fordomain") || (@key[1] eq "fordomain")) {
    $domain = $query{'fordomain'};
    $host = $query{'hostinfo'};
    &gethostinfo($host, $domain);
}
print "</BODY>\n";

sub gethostsbydomain {
    local($domain) = @_;
    open(NIS, "ypcat -d $domain  hosts | sort -bfui +1 2>&1|")
  || warn "Can't run ypcat\n";
    while(<NIS>) {
  if (!/localhost/) {
      ($name, $ip) = split(" ", $_);
      print "<OPTION> $ip\n";
  }
    }
    close(NIS);
}

sub gethostinfo {
    local($h, $d) = @_;

    &getosversion($host);
    &gethardwaretype($host);
    &getinstalledprinters($host);
    &getsoftwarepackages($host);
}
```

```
sub form_begin {
    local($t) = @_;

    print "<CENTER><H3>$t</H3>";
    print "<FORM METHOD=\"POST\" ACTION=\"/~vasa/cgi-bin/bk1\">\n";
}

sub form_end {
    local($cmd) = @_;

    print "<P>";
    print "<INPUT TYPE=submit VALUE=\"$cmd\">\n";
    print "</FORM>";
    print "</CENTER>";
}
```

Our host status CGI is now available to any web browser in the intranet, and it can be further customized and refined to meet the demands of users.

## Summary

In this chapter, we have explored the uses of CGI in the intranet. Using examples, we've looked at how CGI is a versatile and capable tool that provides application functionality to all types of users. We also discussed techniques to overcome the limitations of CGI, such as using the hidden field technique to retain the state in a web browsing session.

Note that we didn't have to worry about client-side, platform-specific application development in our discussion—our efforts are concentrated on the server. By using HTML and CGI, you can quickly provide application functionality to all intranet users, and save time and money in the process.

We've just scratched the surface of CGI, and there are many other potential uses for this technology. For example, CGI is the key to tapping into the wealth of information residing in legacy databases. Using CGI, you can enable access to this information from every web browser-enabled intranet desktop. When coupled with secure connection methods such as SHTTP, CGI can be used to provide employees and management with secure access to sensitive information, such as payroll and human resources information. Other applications include order processing, online surveys, travel requests and authorization, data entry, and so on.

# Appendix

# APPENDIX

# Further Reading

## Web Proxy Services

| | |
|---|---|
| URL | http://www.netscape.com/comprod/server_central/product/proxy/index.htm |
| Description | Describes how to write rules for automatically configuring web proxy services |

## Remote Access Services

| | |
|---|---|
| URL | http://www.internic.net/rfc/rfc1661.txt/ |
| Description | The Request For Comments (RFC) file for the Point-to-Point Protocol (PPP) |
| URL | http://www.windows95.com/connect/dscript.html/ |
| Description | How to use dscript to automate network connection sessions |
| URL | http://www.32bit.com/ |
| Description | How to use RoboDUN to automate network connection sessions |
| URLs | ftp://ftp.cdrom.com/<br>http://www.charm.net/ |
| Description | Winsock application repository |
| URL | http://www.bysnet.com/netsw.html/ |

| | |
|---|---|
| Description | Netswitcher TCP/IP configuration switching utility |
| URL | http://www.sun.com/sunsoft/solstice/Networking-products/PC-X.html/ |
| Description | SunSoft's PC-X X-Windows server software for Windows |
| URL | http://www.graphon.com/ |
| Description | GraphOn's GoGlobal X-Windows server software for Windows |
| URL | http://www.sun.com/sunsoft/solstice/em-products/system/pccache/PCCacheFS.html/ |
| Description | SunSoft's PC-CacheFS caching software for Windows |

## Managing Operating System Software

| | |
|---|---|
| Title | *Automating Solaris Installations*, by Paul Anthony Kasper and Alan L. McClellan, 1995, SunSoft Press. ISBN: 0-13-312505-X |
| Description | Guide to using JumpStart |
| Title | *Microsoft Office Resource Kit for Windows 95 : The Technical Resource for Installing, Configuring, and Supporting Microsoft Office for Windows 95*, 1995, Microsoft Press. ISBN: 1556158181 |
| Description | Guide to Windows installation |

## Managing Software

| | |
|---|---|
| URL | http://www.sun.com/sunsoft/solstice/Networking-products/pcswdir.html/ |
| Description | SunSoft's Solstice PC-Software Director software |
| URL | http://www.sun.com/sunsoft/solstice/Networking-products/PC-Admin.html/ |
| Description | SunSoft's Solstice PC-Admin software |
| URL | http://www.sun.com/sunsoft/solstice/em-products/system/pccache/PCCacheFS.html/ |
| Description | SunSoft's PC-CacheFS caching software for Windows |

## File Sharing

| | |
|---|---|
| URL | http://www.cis.ohio-state.edu/htbin/rfc/rfc1094.html/ |
| Description | The Network File System (NFS) RFC |
| Title | *Managing NFS and NIS*, by Hal Stern. O'Reilly and Associates, Inc. ISBN:0-937175-75-7 |
| Description | Guide to tuning NFS and NIS servers |
| URL | http://www.sun.com/sunsoft/solstice/em-products/system/pccache/PCCacheFS.html/ |
| Description | SunSoft's PC-CacheFS caching software for Windows |
| URL | http://www.sun.com/sunsoft/solaris/desktop/nfs.html/ |
| Description | List of companies that provide NFS software for Windows |
| URLs | http://samba.canberra.edu.au/ news:comp.protocols.smb |
| Description | Samba Windows file server software for UNIX |
| URL | http://www.netapp.com/ |
| Description | Network Appliance file server solutions |
| URL | http://www.sun.com/products-n-solutions/hw/servers/netra/netra_nfs/ |
| Description | Sun's Netra NFS file server solutions |
| URL | http://www.auspex.com/ |
| Description | Auspex NFS file server solutions |

## Domain Name Service (DNS)

| | |
|---|---|
| URL | http://www.internic.net/rfc/rfc1034.txt/ |
| Description | The DNS RFC |
| URL | http://rs0.internic.net/ |
| Description | InterNIC Web site for DNS domain registration |
| Title | *DNS and BIND in a Nutshell*, by Paul Albitz, Cricket Liu. Publishers, O'Reilly & Associates. ISBN: 1565920104 |
| Description | Guide to DNS |
| URL | http://www.dns.net/dnsrd/docs/rfc.html/ |
| Description | DNS-related RFCs |
| URL | http://webdns.lcs.mit.edu/cgi-bin/webdns/about/ |

| Description | Web DNS site |
|---|---|
| URL | http://web.syr.edu/~jmwobus/comfaqs/faq-dns/ |
| Description | DNS Frequently-Asked Questions (FAQ) list |

## E-mail

| URL | http://www.jazzie.com/ii/internet/procmail/ |
|---|---|
| Description | How to use the procmail mail filtering utility |
| URL | http://www.imc.org/imap4/ |
| Description | Interactive Mail Access Protocol (IMAP4) web site |
| URL | http://www.sun.com/sunsoft/solstice/int_mail.html |
| Description | SunSoft's Solstice Internet Mail Server software |

## Multipurpose Internet Mail Extension (MIME)

| URLs | http://www.internic.net/rfc/rfc1521.txt/ <br> http://www.internic.net/rfc/rfc1522.txt/ |
|---|---|
| Description | MIME RFCs |

## Zero-Administration Clients

| URL | http://www.sun.com/sunsoft/solstice/em-products/system/autoclient-wp.html/ |
|---|---|
| Description | SunSoft's Solstice AutoClient technology whitepaper |
| URL | http://www.sun.com/products-n-solutions/hw/servers/netra.html/netra_j/index.html/ |
| Description | Sun's Netra-J JavaStation server solution. |
| URL | http://www.sun.com/javacomputing/ |
| Description | Sun Java Computing Web site |
| URL | http://officeforjava.corel.com/ |
| Description | Corel Office for Java Web site |
| Description | GraphOn's X-Windows server software for JavaStations |
| URL | http://www.graphon.com/ |

## Web Services

| | |
|---|---|
| URL | http://www.microsoft.com/msword/internet/ia/ |
| Description | Microsoft Internet Assistant Web publishing software |
| URL | http://www.adobe.com/prodindex/framemaker/ |
| Description | Adobe FrameMaker Web publishing software |
| URL | http://home.mcom.com/comprod/mirror/client_download.html/ |
| Description | Netscape Communications Navigator Gold Web publishing software |
| URL | http://www.netobjects.com/ |
| Description | NetObjects Fusion Web publishing/site management software |
| URL | http://www.yahoo.com/Computers_and_Internet/Software/Internet/World_Wide_Web/Servers/ |
| Description | List of World Wide Web (WWW) server software |
| URL | http://www.apache.org/ |
| Description | Apache Web server software site |
| URL | http://www.apache.org/docs/FAQ.html |
| Description | Apache Web server FAQ |
| URL | http://hoohoo.ncsa.uiuc.edu/ |
| Description | NCSA Web server software site |
| URL | http://www.w3.org/pub/WWW/Daemon/ |
| Description | W3C Web server software site |
| URL | http://home.mcom.com/comprod/mirror/server_download.html/ |
| Description | Netscape Communications web server software site |

## Common Gateway Interface (CGI)

| | |
|---|---|
| URL | http://hoohoo.ncsa.uiuc.edu/cgi/env.html |
| Description | List of environment variables available to a CGI program |
| Title | *Programming Perl*, by Larry Wall, ISBN: 0-937175-64-1 |
| Description | Guide to Perl programming |
| URL | http://scwww.ucs.indiana.edu/FAQ/Perl/index.html |

| | |
|---|---|
| Description | Perl FAQ |
| URL | http://www.ncsa.uiuc.edu/SDG/Software/Mosaic/Docs/fill-out-forms/overview.html |
| Description | Information about HTML form directives |

# Index